THE
FAITH

PARTICIPANT'S GUIDE

Also by Charles Colson

Born Again

Loving God

Kingdoms in Conflict

Against the Night

Why America Doesn't Work (with Jack Eckerd)

The Body (with Ellen Santilli Vaughn)

Gideon's Torch (with Ellen Vaughn)

How Now Shall We Live? (with Nancy Pearcey)

Being the Body (with Ellen Santilli Vaughn)

God and Government

The Good Life (with Harold Fickett)

The Faith (with Harold Fickett)

Resources by Garry Poole

The Complete Book of Questions

Seeker Small Groups

The Three Habits of Highly Contagious Christians

In the Tough Questions series:

Don't All Religions Lead to God?

How Could God Allow Suffering and Evil?

How Does Anyone Know God Exists?

Why Become a Christian?

Tough Questions Leader's Guide (with Judson Poling)

THE
FAITH

PARTICIPANT'S GUIDE

Six Sessions

CHARLES COLSON
AND GARRY POOLE

ZONDERVAN®

ZONDERVAN.com/
AUTHORTRACKER
follow your favorite authors

The authors wish to express their gratitude to Laura Allen
for her outstanding writing and editing contributions.
Laura's creative insights took this guide to the next level.

The Faith Participant's Guide
Copyright © 2008 by Charles W. Colson

Requests for information should be addressed to:

Zondervan, *Grand Rapids, Michigan* 49530

ISBN 978-0-310-27607-4

Interior design by Beth Shagene

Printed in the United States of America

12 13 14 • 25 24 23 22 21 20 19 18 17 16 15 14 13 12 11 10 9 8 7 6 5

CONTENTS

The past not only shapes the present; it can also show us the future. We can see much further ahead by standing on the shoulders of those who have gone before us. This discussion guide is dedicated to upholding the faith that was "once for all entrusted to the saints"—those essentials that all true Christians have always believed, and what C. S. Lewis called "mere Christianity." It's our deep conviction that this faith is what Christians need to live out and defend in the midst of the extraordinary challenges of our time.

THE FAITH —
GIVEN ONCE, FOR ALL

Christianity fails today because it isn't being explained. It isn't being explained because people don't know what they believe. They don't know why they believe it and they don't know why it matters.

Charles Colson

Before You Begin

This session is planned for 50 minutes, including two DVD segments and 12 discussion questions (some of which also include follow-up questions). If time is a constraint, feel free to select only those questions most pertinent to your group discussion.

The synopsis preceding each question or questions is designed to provide a short summary of the content covered by that question or questions. During your group time, we encourage you to read the Scripture(s) together. While it is not necessary to read the summaries during the meeting, your group will be better prepared to take the discussion to a deeper level if you are able to read and meditate on them in advance.

Make every effort to read the prologue and chapters 1–4 of the book *The Faith* prior to the session. These corresponding chapters provide a more in-depth explanation of the concepts addressed in this session's DVD segments, the summary sections, and the group discussion questions that follow.

DVD Teaching Segment (20 minutes)

Notes

Christianity is a worldview — a system of life and thought

There is a God and God is

God has given us truth and it is knowable

God has revealed himself in the Scriptures

Deeds versus creeds

DVD Group Discussion (25 minutes)

Everywhere, Always, by All

> *Jude, a servant of Jesus Christ and a brother of James, to those who have been called, who are loved by God the Father and kept by Jesus Christ: Mercy, peace and love be yours in abundance. Dear friends, although I was very eager to write to you about the salvation we share, I felt I had to write and urge you to contend for the faith that was once for all entrusted to the saints.*
>
> Jude 1 – 3

Most professing Christians don't know what they believe, and so can neither understand nor defend the Christian faith — much less live it. Many of the things we tell nonbelievers do not represent real Christianity. And most nonbelievers draw their impressions of the Christian faith from the stereotypes and caricatures that popular culture produces. The challenge of anti-theism and radical Islam could not come at a worse time for the Church, because most Christians do not understand what they believe, why they believe it, and why it matters.

1 **In what ways is Christianity misunderstood by the non-Christian world and why is this a problem for the Church? How is our culture's definition of Christianity a poor representation of orthodox Christian beliefs?**

Orthodoxy

We must pay more careful attention, therefore, to what we have heard, so that we do not drift away. For if the message spoken by angels was binding, and every violation and disobedience received its just punishment, how shall we escape if we ignore such a great salvation? This salvation, which was first announced by the Lord, was confirmed to us by those who heard him. God also testified to it by signs, wonders and various miracles, and gifts of the Holy Spirit distributed according to his will.

Hebrews 2:1–4

It may seem odd to rely on the ancient roots of Christianity at a time when progress is so exalted. But progress does not always mean discovering something new. Sometimes it means rediscovering wisdom that is ancient and eternal. We all find our identity in our roots. Visit nearly any family and you'll see pictures of grandparents and earlier generations. People go to great lengths to trace their ancestry. Adopted children seek their birth parents. Where we come from tells us who we are, and so it is in the Church.

We call the core beliefs that have united Christians through the ages *orthodoxy*, or "right belief." Understanding this faith, once entrusted for all, is critically important today, for we live in a time when Christians and the beliefs they uphold are under assault.

If we are to face today's grave threats to the Christian Church, we must look across the sweep of Christian communions, Protestant, Catholic, and Orthodox, to find the original consensus of the early Church; that is, those essential elements of our faith that, from the beginning, all true Christians have believed.

2 **What is meant by "Christian orthodoxy"? Why is it absolutely essential for Christians to understand our biblical and historical roots?**

Competing Worldviews

So I tell you this, and insist on it in the Lord, that you must no longer live as the Gentiles do, in the futility of their thinking. They are darkened in their understanding and separated from the life of God because of the ignorance that is in them due to the hardening of their hearts.

Ephesians 4:17 – 18

So then, just as you received Christ Jesus as Lord, continue to live in him, rooted and built up in him, strengthened in the faith as you were taught, and overflowing with thankfulness. See to it that no one takes you captive through hollow and deceptive philosophy, which depends on human tradition and the basic principles of this world rather than on Christ.

Colossians 2:6 – 8

Everybody has a worldview ... some basic premises that you think about life and you say, "Ah, that informs what I do and how I see things." Christians must see that the faith is more than a religion or even a relationship with Jesus; the faith is a complete view of the world and humankind's place in it. Christianity is a worldview that speaks to every area of life, and its foundational doctrines define its content. If we don't know what we believe — even what Christianity is — how can we live it and defend it? Our ignorance is crippling us.

3 Do you agree that we all, Christians or not, go through life with a worldview that informs everything we think, say, and do? Why or why not? What is the basis of your worldview? Explain.

4 In what ways is Christianity—and the Western civilization it helped build—under assault by the aggressive anti-Christian worldviews of secularism (anti-theism) and radical Islam? Does this matter? Why or why not?

God Is

The heavens declare the glory of God; the skies proclaim the work of his hands. Day after day they pour forth speech; night after night they display knowledge. There is no speech or language where their voice is not heard.

Psalm 19:1–3

One of the Christian faith's most persuasive contemporary critics is Sam Harris, who articulates the powerful doubts that we all recognize in our moments of soul searching. In his book *Letter to a Christian Nation*, he wondered what God was doing when hurricane Katrina devastated New Orleans and how sad it was that people there died praying to an "imaginary friend."

My thoughts have been as dark at times. During one of those times I was at a friend's home in western North Carolina. One morning I got up early and was greeted by the magnificent sight of the Blue Ridge Mountains rising out of the mist, the sun throwing the shadows of the lower peaks against the higher summits, the foliage glistening with dew. There was no explanation for what I was seeing—the intricate details of nature, genuine beauty–apart from a creator God. This could not be an illusion, an accident, or the result of some random process. While the other planets are sterile and lifeless, this one throbs with life and beauty. *God is.* I knew God exists at a deeper level than I had ever known anything in my life before. His existence didn't depend on my feelings, either. I might feel desperate, weary of praying, ready to throw in the towel, but God still is. There is no other explanation for reality. What I saw, I realized, was the answer to what I had thought were unanswered prayers.

5 Do you agree that our view of Christianity must move beyond a very individualized, personal relationship that is "between me and God," to the realization that "God is" no matter the circumstances? Why or why not? What dangers lurk behind a belief system that rests primarily on personal experience or feelings?

God Has Spoken

All Scripture is God-breathed and is useful for teaching, rebuking, correcting and training in righteousness, so that the man of God may be thoroughly equipped for every good work.

2 Timothy 3:16–17

Above all, you must understand that no prophecy of Scripture came about by the prophet's own interpretation. For prophecy never had its origin in the will of man, but men spoke from God as they were carried along by the Holy Spirit.

2 Peter 1:20–21

Simply put, the Bible is the rock on which the Church stands or falls. It is the ultimate authority for all Christians—Protestants, Catholics, and Orthodox alike. It is revealed propositional truth. The texts were written by men under the inspiration of the Holy Spirit, and thus are revealed to us. It is propositional because it makes a series of claims. It is truth because it is from God, and thus must certainly be true; God could not have spoken something that is not true because that would be contrary to His nature. This is why all true Christians take the Bible as their ultimate authority — and why no Christian should ever be hesitant to defend it.

6 How important to one's faith is one's attitude toward God's Word? What hinders you from learning, applying, and defending the doctrines and truths found in the Scriptures?

Absolute Truth

"You are a king, then!" said Pilate. Jesus answered, "You are right in saying I am a king. In fact, for this reason I was born, and for this I came into the world, to testify to the truth. Everyone on the side of truth listens to me."
                                                                    John 18:37

Jesus answered, "I am the way and the truth and the life. No one comes to the Father except through me. If you really knew me, you would know my Father as well. From now on, you do know him and have seen him."
                                                                    John 14:6 – 7

The question of truth — of a common and knowable reality that exists independently of our perception — is the great fault line of Western culture today. The dominant point of view dismisses the idea. The fastest way to provoke scorn from most university professors is to use the words *reality, truth,* and most of all *absolute truth.* Why does this view of truth breed such animosity? Because rebellious human nature resists truth's claims. If something is really true, it must be true not just for the person saying it but for the person hearing it. And the fact is, we don't want to obey a higher authority from any quarter—especially what purports to be from God—for fear it will impinge upon our personal autonomy. We cling to the idea that we create our own truth.

7 In what ways does our postmodern culture deny objective truth? Fifty-four percent of evangelical Christians believe there's no such thing as *absolute truth*. What do you say? Give reasons for your response.

8 Is it logically consistent to believe in the revealed Jesus of Scripture and the absolute claims he makes, and at the same time deny that absolute truth exists? Why or why not?

Truth versus Tolerance

In the presence of God and of Christ Jesus, who will judge the living and the dead, and in view of his appearing and his kingdom, I give you this charge: Preach the Word; be prepared in season and out of season; correct, rebuke and encourage — with great patience and careful instruction. For the time will come when men will not put up with sound doctrine. Instead, to suit their own desires, they will gather around them a great number of teachers to say what their itching ears want to hear. They will turn their ears away from the truth and turn aside to myths.

2 Timothy 4:1–4

What Jesus teaches is that reality is not what we subjectively make of it, or what our culture may believe. There is objective truth, and we are able to apprehend it with our senses. We are not a dream in the mind of God, an illusion, as Eastern religions and some New Age philosophies teach.

What's really at issue here is a dramatic shift in the prevailing belief of Western cultural elites; we have come into a postmodern era that rejects the idea of truth itself. If there is no such thing as truth, then Christianity's claims are inherently offensive and even bigoted against others. Tolerance, falsely defined as putting all propositions on an equal footing — as opposed to giving all ideas an equal hearing — has replaced truth.

9 **How has a false definition of "tolerance" replaced a desire for "truth" in Western culture? How is this loss of truth offensive to God?**

10 How is the postmodern world's pressure toward "political correctness" and "tolerance" silencing Christians and Christianity today? Share an occasion when you feared being seen as bigoted or offensive by others because of your biblical beliefs. How did you handle the situation?

Deeds ... Not Creeds?

In the beginning was the Word, and the Word was with God, and the Word was God. He was with God in the beginning. Through him all things were made; without him nothing was made that has been made.

John 1:1 – 3

This distaste for doctrine has led some postmodern Christians to adopt the mantra, "We want deeds not creeds." But wait a minute. For over thirty years, the movement known as Prison Fellowship has been taking the Gospel into the prisons, demonstrating the transforming power of Christ to turn the most reviled sinners into saints. No one would argue that these have not been worthwhile deeds. But if the creeds we believe in are false, then our efforts have been totally misplaced; we cannot be sure that our deeds, however noble, are really good. It is the creed that makes us carry out the deed — that keeps us going into the most rotten holes in the world—and gives us the message we preach. The same is true of any Christian movement based on faith.

11 Why must our good deeds be the fruit of our creeds, even if the result is the same?

12 Why do you think it is important for Christians to correctly defend and live out the essential doctrines of the faith that have been entrusted to us, and what are some of the potential consequences of not doing so?

DVD Closing Segment and Prayer (5 minutes)

Use the space provided below to take notes on anything that stands out to you.

Before the Next Session

Choose one or more of the following ways to further digest and apply the concepts and principles you're learning:

• **Set aside some alone time to prayerfully reflect and meditate on the material covered in this session.** You might wish to review all of the summary sections preceding each question, or select the particular Scripture verses and corresponding synopsis you feel God is leading you to study. As you meditate and focus on God's Word, let his truth fill you. And as you pray and invite the Holy Spirit to transform and renew your mind, consider what God may be teaching you. What new insights have you discovered; what fresh perspectives have you gained; how might you apply these things to your everyday life? Use the space below to journal these things.

- **Meet with one or two other people from your group to further discuss how you might apply what you're learning to your everyday life.** Share with one another what has impacted you and how God is especially speaking to you. Discuss what concepts or topics have been particularly difficult for you to understand or accept. Also be sure to set aside some time to pray together.

- **Initiate a dialogue with someone who is not a participant in your group.** Invite a friend who is not yet a Christian to interact with you over some of the concepts you have been covering in the book, DVD clips, and group discussion. Be especially careful to listen with a sincere desire to hear and understand what your friend believes and why. Ask your friend if he or she would be interested in hearing some of the ways you've been impacted by your study of the material. You may wish to share some of the insights you gained from your conversation with the rest of your group when you meet again.

Also, in preparation for session two, please read chapters 5 – 6 of the book *The Faith*.

WHAT WENT RIGHT, WHAT WENT WRONG

This is why the cross is the symbol of Christianity. It marks the dividing line between man's futile effort to achieve God's righteousness and God's gracious act in sending Christ to redeem all who will follow. It represents the most decisive moment in history, when God answered the great human dilemma that we have all sinned and yearn for forgiveness: God took upon Himself our sins to set us free. It is where justice and mercy meet.

Charles Colson

Before You Begin

This session is planned for 50 minutes, including two DVD segments and 12 discussion questions (some of which also include follow-up questions). If time is a constraint, feel free to select only those questions most pertinent to your group discussion.

The synopsis preceding each question or questions is designed to provide a short summary of the content covered by that question or questions. During your group time, we encourage you to read the Scripture(s) together. While it is not necessary to read the summaries during the meeting, your group will be better prepared to take the discussion to a deeper level if you are able to read and meditate on them in advance.

Make every effort to read chapters 5–6 of the book *The Faith* prior to the session. These corresponding chapters provide a more in-depth explanation of the concepts addressed in this session's DVD segments, the summary sections, and the group discussion questions that follow.

DVD Teaching Segment (20 minutes)

Notes

The coherence of the Christian story

Creation: A test of free will

The Fall: A death sentence

Redemption: The substitionary atoning death of Christ

Restoration: The kingdom of God has invaded planet earth

DVD Group Discussion (25 minutes)

What Went Right, What Went Wrong — The Creation and the Fall

In the beginning God created the heavens and the earth. Now the earth was formless and empty, darkness was over the surface of the deep, and the Spirit of God was hovering over the waters. And God said, "Let there be light," and there was light. . . . God saw all that he had made, and it was very good.

Genesis 1:1 – 3, 31

Originally, God's creation was unspoiled; the Garden of Eden was an earthly paradise for our first parents, Adam and Eve. But something terrible happened to disrupt this earthly paradise.

The Bible teaches that human history is actually a subplot of a larger story — the cosmic war in the heavens between God and Satan, good and evil. Satan rebelled against God before the world began, which God defeated, throwing Satan and his followers out of heaven (Isaiah 14:12 – 15). But the war in heaven continued on earth. Satan, in the form of a serpent, approached Eve in the Garden of Eden. His first words raised doubts about God's word (the same challenge we hear today). "Did God really say, 'You must not eat from any tree in the garden'?" the serpent asks (Genesis 3:1). In this way the human race inherited a legacy of sin, both in the world itself and in human nature. Adam and Eve set the pattern for the whole human race; human nature was thereafter bent toward sin. We are born as sinners. Everything from the time of Adam has been stained and corrupted by forbidden fruit, including the human soul.

1 Christianity is a cohesive and compelling four-part story that explains all of reality: *Creation, the Fall, Redemption, and Restoration.* Why is it important to begin the story with God's original plan for creation in order to more fully grasp the consequences of the Fall? And what's the significance in continuing the story beyond Redemption to Restoration?

The Problem of Evil

> To Adam he said, "Because you listened to your wife and ate from the tree
> about which I commanded you, 'You must not eat of it,' Cursed is the ground
> because of you; through painful toil you will eat of it all the days of your life.
> It will produce thorns and thistles for you, and you will eat the plants of the
> field. By the sweat of your brow you will eat your food until you return to the
> ground, since from it you were taken; for dust you are and to dust you will
> return."
>
> Genesis 3:17–19

Why would God bring a world into existence that would be characterized by evil and suffering? What about "acts of God" like hurricanes, tsunamis, floods, and famine? Humanity is afflicted with cancer and a thousand other diseases. Can all the evil of the world be attributed to humankind's failings? Is God truly innocent? He put Adam and Eve in a situation where He knew, if God is omniscient, or all-knowing, that they would fail. This is the question Sam Harris and other atheists have raised. It is called the problem of evil. Theologians and philosophers have wrestled with this question from the beginning of time — and will continue to do so. How could a good God allow all the sin and suffering in the world?

2 **Does God's curse upon sin seem unusually harsh to you? Why or why not? Who do you think is ultimately responsible for the suffering and evil in the world? Give reasons for your response.**

HUMAN BEINGS MUST HAVE FREE WILL
TO BECOME FULLY FORMED BEINGS, TO
MAXIMIZE OUR POTENTIAL, ETC. THE GIFT OF
FREE WILL MEANS WE CAN & WILL MAKE
BAD CHOICES (SIN) TOO. WITH SIN COMES
CONSEQUENCES, UNHEALTHY FOOD, PRIDEFUL
LOOTING OF HUMES.
SO — IF EVERY SINGLE HUMAN BEING WAS
PERFECT WOULD THE WORLD BE PERFECT?
PRETTY DARN CLOSE!

Satan's Best Work

And there was war in heaven. Michael and his angels fought against the dragon, and the dragon and his angels fought back. But he was not strong enough, and they lost their place in heaven. The great dragon was hurled down — that ancient serpent called the devil, or Satan, who leads the whole world astray. He was hurled to the earth, and his angels with him. . . . Therefore rejoice, you heavens and you who dwell in them! But woe to the earth and the sea, because the devil has gone down to you! He is filled with fury, because he knows that his time is short.

Revelation 12:7–9, 12

Satan practices his deception not only on individuals but on whole cultures. He uses false religions and false ideas to ensnare cultures in evil. If he can turn a whole people group toward worshiping a false god, he can compromise millions of consciences at once. The most tragic instances of this phenomenon come in the form of otherwise decent men and women carrying out crimes against humanity. Hitler was a monster, but the Nazi war machine and the Holocaust death camps were run by thousands upon thousands of normal Germans. Ordinary people also carried out the Turks' genocide against the Armenians, ran the Soviet Gulag and China's Cultural Revolution, Pol Pot's Killing Fields, and the Rwandan genocide. Those who are currently killing people by the hundreds of thousands in Darfur or blowing themselves up in the Middle East are as human as we are. In our own country slavery turned otherwise good Christians' hearts to stone, which continued to manifest itself in segregation and today's racial divisions. With questions like "Did God really say . . . ?" and "What is truth?" a thousand devils have been let loose upon us, and we have danced along.

3 What role did Satan play in the fall of man? What role does he continue to play in ensnaring entire cultures in the cosmic battle between good and evil? (See Ephesians 2:1–3; 6:12.)

Human Responsibility and Denial

> *Therefore, just as sin entered the world through one man, and death through*
> *sin, and in this way death came to all men, because all sinned.*
>
> Romans 5:12

The truth is we are responsible. All true Christians affirm that humans, given the gift of a free will from God, disobeyed Him. Our original parents' sin is thus our legacy. It is critical to understand why Christians believe this. Besides the biblical witness, the history of civilization along with our own experience attests to it. And why does it matter? Get this wrong and you get life wrong. Human responsibility is misunderstood, chaos results, and human hubris leads to tragically flawed utopian experiments. And you get God wrong because without human responsibility there is no need for a Savior. These questions are critical to understanding life and reality.

4 **What are the possible consequences of a worldview that denies human responsibility for bad moral choices and embraces the view we are all just victims of our upbringing? How does this result in a distorted view of life, reality, and even God? In what ways have you been held captive by this way of thinking?**

A CONSEQUENCE OF VICTIMHOOD IS THE LIMIT IT PUTS ON A PERSON. YOU CANNOT MAXIMIZE YOUR POTENTIAL IF YOU BELIEVE OUTSIDE FORCES DETERMINE YOUR OWN OUTCOME.

T

Human Free Will

> *The LORD God took the man and put him in the Garden of Eden to work it*
> *and take care of it. And the LORD God commanded the man, "You are free*
> *to eat from any tree in the garden; but you must not eat from the tree of the*
> *knowledge of good and evil, for when you eat of it you will surely die."*
>
> Genesis 2:15 – 17

Knowing that humankind could freely choose to sin, should God have created us as free creatures? Was this worth the untold suffering of human history? As we ponder this question, consider whether we enjoy being free-willed creatures. Would we rather exchange our place in the creation for that of the finest among the other animals, say a dolphin, a lion, or an eagle? Would we choose to live only by instinct? We certainly want the blessings of free will, even if we don't like the consequences of our evil choices, for which we often perversely blame God. But of course we can't have it both ways.

5 Why did God create us with free will when he knew it would result in our rebellion, with evil and suffering as its necessary consequence? What are the pros and cons of free will?

The Incarnation — God Made Flesh

Your attitude should be the same as that of Christ Jesus: Who, being in very nature God, did not consider equality with God something to be grasped, but made himself nothing, taking the very nature of a servant, being made in human likeness. And being found in appearance as a man, he humbled himself and became obedient to death—even death on a cross!

Philippians 2:5–8

Here then is the scandal. God chose to invade planet earth in the person of His Son, what Christians call the Incarnation—God becomes flesh. For many, including Joseph, the doctrine of the Virgin Birth is hard to accept. But the God who could speak the universe into being, who could create human life, could certainly choose to make Himself known by the power of the Holy Spirit through a virgin. And it was essential He do it this way. Jesus could never have been the Savior of humankind if He were born into sin, because then His death on the cross would be for His *own* sins, not for *ours* alone. Only a totally sinless savior could take our sins upon Himself, which means God, and only God, could be His Father.

6 **Why is the virgin birth an essential part of God's plan for the redemption of sinful people? What questions or issues does the incarnation raise for you?**

The Invasion

> "The Spirit of the Lord is on me, because he has anointed me to preach good news to the poor. He has sent me to proclaim freedom for the prisoners and recovery of sight for the blind, to release the oppressed, to proclaim the year of the Lord's favor." Then [Jesus] rolled up the scroll, gave it back to the attendant and sat down. The eyes of everyone in the synagogue were fastened on him, and he began by saying to them, "Today this scripture is fulfilled in your hearing."
>
> Luke 4:18–21

Sometimes I think Jesus' humble announcement of the liberation of the people and the coming of the Kingdom of God is as badly misunderstood in churches today as it was by the Jews of His time. He was bringing in the reign of God on earth—first through His own ministry and then by establishing a peaceful occupying force, His Church, which would carry on God's redemption until Christ's return in power and glory at the Kingdom's final triumph. In the cosmic struggle of good and evil, Jesus' inauguration of the Kingdom was more decisive than D-Day or any other invasion in human history. The revolutionary nature of God's invasion of our world is far more significant than all the other invasions of history taken together.

This one established the possibility and opportunity of the rule of God in every human heart and began the reclamation of our world as God's own.

7 **What is your overall reaction to this idea that God has invaded our planet to set up his kingdom as a peaceful occupying force known as the Church? In what ways might this understanding of the role of the Church impact the way you'll view and participate in church in the future?**

The Crucifixion and Resurrection

For what I received I passed on to you as of first importance: that Christ died for our sins according to the Scriptures, that he was buried, that he was raised on the third day according to the Scriptures, and that he appeared to Peter, and then to the Twelve. After that, he appeared to more than five hundred of the brothers at the same time.

1 Corinthians 15:3–6

But if it is preached that Christ has been raised from the dead, how can some of you say that there is no resurrection of the dead? If there is no resurrection of the dead, then not even Christ has been raised. And if Christ has not been raised, our preaching is useless and so is your faith.

1 Corinthians 15:12–14

Jesus' story doesn't end at the cross or the tomb. For Christ was bodily raised from the dead, and He lives and reigns today, seated at the right hand of the Father. The ugly crucifixion, the most hideous symbol of death and shame ever devised, was converted in that instant into the holiest of holy symbols. All true Christians believe that Jesus Christ has been bodily raised in victory over death. Without the resurrection, Jesus is no different than any other prophet or Buddha. This is why the central attack on Christianity has always been against the scandal of the cross and the empty tomb.

8 Why was it necessary for Jesus to live a sinless life but to die a sinner's death? What did his crucifixion accomplish?

PG4) THE ONLY SINLESS MAN WAS ABLE
TO TAKE ON HUMANITY'S SINS.

¢ THIS IS A BIG QUESTION — NOT
REALLY SURE I UNDERSTAND THE CONCEPT!

9 Why is the resurrection the linchpin upon which Christianity turns and thus the point of greatest attack by others?

The Ascension—Christ Lives and Reigns

So when they met together, they asked him, "Lord, are you at this time going to restore the kingdom to Israel?" He said to them: "It is not for you to know the times or dates the Father has set by his own authority. But you will receive power when the Holy Spirit comes on you; and you will be my witnesses in Jerusalem, and in all Judea and Samaria, and to the ends of the earth." After he said this, he was taken up before their very eyes, and a cloud hid him from their sight. They were looking intently up into the sky as he was going, when suddenly two men dressed in white stood beside them. "Men of Galilee," they said, "why do you stand here looking into the sky? This same

Jesus, who has been taken from you into heaven, will come back in the same way you have seen him go into heaven."

Acts 1:6–11

Jesus' ascension is a crucial event in God's redemption of creation—God's reclaiming of the world from Satan. The ascension is a preview, in many senses, of God's ultimate victory, as the angels who explain Christ's ascent into heaven also prophesy that in the same way—in glory and power—Christ will return to the earth (Acts 1:11). In the ascendant Christ we see what we shall one day be—persons with immortal bodies who are brought into God's presence. Christ's ascension also ensured that the Holy Spirit would be sent as our advocate and comforter, through whose indwelling presence believers have continuous access to Christ, who is now seated at the right hand of the Father where He continues to act on our behalf.

10 **The following chart summarizes some biblical references associated with the ascension. Select one concept that most inspires or encourages you, and tell why.**

John 16:6–7	Jesus' departure ensured he would send the Counselor, or Holy Spirit, to aid believers.
Hebrews 1:1–3; 4:14–16	Jesus is now at the right hand of God and is sustaining all things.
Hebrews 7:24–26	Jesus, as a permanent priest, now intercedes on behalf of his followers.
Acts 1:9–11	Jesus will one day return in the same way that he ascended.
1 Corinthians 15:50–53	Believers will one day be given immortal bodies similar to the body Jesus had when he ascended.

Another challenging event for me to internalize! But — the fact that Jesus spent back on earth with his disciples does seem or foreshadow his coming to be present with us more. So, for certain about. I don't know that he returns in the 'same way' but he can be an earthly presence.

God's Kingdom on Earth

"This, then, is how you should pray: 'Our Father in heaven, hallowed
be your name, your kingdom come, your will be done on earth as it is in
heaven.'"

Matthew 6:9–10

After John was put in prison, Jesus went into Galilee, proclaiming the good
news of God. "The time has come," he said. "The kingdom of God is near.
Repent and believe the good news!"

Mark 1:14–15

Every night I pray, "Help me, Lord, to advance your Kingdom." It's more than just "Help me to be a good Christian" or "Help me to have a closer relationship with you." Those things are important, but the fullness of the good news is when I am acting in such a way that I advance His Kingdom. Everything we should be doing should be pre-figuring the Kingdom that will come on Jesus' return.

11 **Jesus proclaimed, "The kingdom of God is at hand." In what new and practical ways can you participate in the activity of advancing his kingdom right here and now?**

- MAKE MORE CLEAN TO MY KIDS WHAT MY FAITH SHOWS ME, WHAT WE BELIEVE, HOW IS FAITHFUL LIFE BEAUTIFUL AND & HOW MY DOUBB & CHALLENGS.

- DO NOT BE SHY IN TELLING OTHERS ABOUT THIS JOURNEY...

12 From what you've learned thus far, briefly summarize each component of the Christian story: *Creation, the Fall, Redemption,* and *Restoration.* Which part of the story has most impacted you during this session? Why?

DVD Closing Segment and Prayer (5 minutes)

Use the space provided below to take notes on anything that stands out to you.

Before the Next Session

Choose one or more of the following ways to further digest and apply the concepts and principles you're learning:

• **Set aside some alone time to prayerfully reflect and meditate on the material covered in this session.** You might wish to review all of the summary sections preceding each question, or select the particular Scripture verses and corresponding synopsis you feel God is leading you to study. As you meditate and focus on God's Word, let his truth fill you. And as you pray and invite the Holy Spirit to transform and renew your mind, consider what God may be teaching you. What new insights have you discovered; what fresh perspectives have you gained; how might you apply these things to your everyday life? Use the space below to journal these things.

- **Meet with one or two other people from your group to further discuss how you might apply what you're learning to your everyday life.** Share with one another what has impacted you and how God is especially speaking to you. Discuss what concepts or topics have been particularly difficult for you to understand or accept. Also be sure to set aside some time to pray together.

- **Initiate a dialogue with someone who is not a participant in your group.** Invite a friend who is not yet a Christian to interact with you over some of the concepts you have been covering in the book, DVD clips, and group discussion. Be especially careful to listen with a sincere desire to hear and understand what your friend believes and why. Ask your friend if he or she would be interested in hearing some of the ways you've been impacted by your study of the material. You may wish to share some of the insights you gained from your conversation with the rest of your group when you meet again.

Also, in preparation for session three, please read chapters 8–9 of the book *The Faith.*

THE FREE GIFT — COSTLY GRACE

To endure the cross is not tragedy; it is the suffering which is the fruit of an exclusive allegiance to Jesus Christ. . . . Only he who believes is obedient and only he who is obedient believes.

Dietrich Bonhoeffer

Make us worthy, Lord, to serve our fellow men throughout the world who live and die in poverty and hunger. Give them through our hands their daily bread, and by our understanding love, give peace and joy.

Mother Teresa

Before You Begin

This session is planned for 50 minutes, including two DVD segments and 12 discussion questions (some of which also include follow-up questions). If time is a constraint, feel free to select only those questions most pertinent to your group discussion.

The synopsis preceding each question or questions is designed to provide a short summary of the content covered by that question or questions. During your group time, we encourage you to read the Scripture(s) together. While it is not necessary to read the summaries during the meeting, your group will be better prepared to take the discussion to a deeper level if you are able to read and meditate on them in advance.

Make every effort to read chapters 8–9 of the book *The Faith* prior to the session. These corresponding chapters provide a more in-depth explanation of the concepts addressed in this session's DVD segments, the summary sections, and the group discussion questions that follow.

DVD Teaching Segment (20 minutes)

Notes
Understanding God's grace

Saved to do works of righteousness

Suffering is inherent in the Christian faith

Christianity commands forgiveness and reconciliation

The scandal of the cross versus the scandal of division

DVD Group Discussion (25 minutes)

Saving Faith

> *But the other criminal rebuked him. "Don't you fear God," he said, "since*
> *you are under the same sentence? We are punished justly, for we are getting*
> *what our deeds deserve. But this man has done nothing wrong." Then*
> *he said, "Jesus, remember me when you come into your kingdom." Jesus*
> *answered him, "I tell you the truth, today you will be with me in paradise."*
>
> Luke 23:40–43

I ask inmates to put themselves in the place of the good thief and to pray just as He prayed, "Jesus, You're innocent. You're holy. I'm guilty. Remember me." The good thief's understanding of his own sin, his repentance, and his desire to be with Jesus made it possible for him to be saved — and for Jesus to answer his prayer. Repentance and the desire to be in Jesus' company are the crucial elements of any sincere conversion. Thousands of times around the world I have seen the power of God work in the most remarkable ways through such simple prayers, whole groups of inmates and the poor praying out loud, individuals weeping, many responding with open confessions of faith. I have seen some of the hardest, toughest, meanest looking convicts dissolve in a flood of tears. In some prisons, I have literally been mobbed afterward by weeping convicts. They get it. Repentance and acceptance of Christ's saving work bring with them a new understanding of one's own worth that at first may seem paradoxical. However gravely I have sinned, Christ still thought I was worthy of His sacrifice. That's grace, indeed; that's love!

1 **Why is it that we cannot truly become open to Christ's offer of forgiveness and our own true worth until we realize the depth of our sin? What hinders us from admitting our own depravity and need?**

PRIDE.

1. WE WANT TO THINK OF OURSELVES A 'GOOD'. EVEN WHEN WE CONFESS BEING SINNERS DON'T WE (I!) THINK — "BUT NOT THAT BAD OF A SINNER" . . . .

2. WE DON'T WANT TO ADMIT TO A LACK OF CONTROL. I HAVE ENOUGH CONTROL OVER CONDITIONS OF MY LIFE — MONEY, HEALTH, KIDS, TO GIVE THE ILLUSION OF CONTROL. I PRAY TO UNDERSTAND THIS IS NOT MY OWN WITHOUT SOME THING EVER TO POINT IT OUT.

2 Do you agree that true repentance (turning away from sin) and the desire to be in Jesus' company are the crucial elements of any sincere conversion? Why or why not? Briefly share what this looks like in your own life.

A Free Gift—Faith Alone

For it is by grace you have been saved, through faith—and this not from yourselves, it is the gift of God—not by works, so that no one can boast.

Ephesians 2:8–9

The New Testament makes it clear that this gift of salvation, becoming righteous, or exchanging identities comes by faith—not works—or any merit of our own (Ephesians 2:8). Since the Gospel seems so clear and inviting, why do so many resist the Good News? Part of the answer is that salvation, being a free gift from God, sounds too easy. Certainly God wouldn't just let us into heaven because we embraced Christ's saving message, without regard to our own past behavior. That's counterintuitive. We also like the good things we do, and we think we ought to get credit for them. We'd prefer to save ourselves, a preference that stems from pride. The sin of the Garden of Eden is the very thing that still condemns us. People also resist the Good News because they fail to take sin seriously. If we're really not sinners, they seem to think, then all we need is a little self-improvement. But when we do take our sin seriously—when we realize we have been rescued from a hopeless condition—dead in our sins and trespasses—then we rejoice and in gratitude join God in reclaiming the world He loves for Himself. We'll want others to know about this incredible free gift as well.

3 **What does it mean to be saved by faith alone? How and when do "good works" figure in? Why does it appear so difficult for many people to receive the free gift that Jesus offers?**

An Exchange of Identities

I have been crucified with Christ and I no longer live, but Christ lives in me. The life I live in the body, I live by faith in the Son of God, who loved me and gave himself for me.

Galatians 2:20

To live as Christians, we must first understand exactly what occurred on the cross when the good thief expressed faith in Christ and Christ promised him eternity. It was an exchange of identities. Christ comes to the cross to die, giving His righteous life for us; we in turn come to the cross to die, surrendering our old sinful life for Him. Thereafter Christ lives in us (Galatians 2:20). This is the heart of Christian conversion. It is what we mean by the term *salvation*, or what Christians frequently speak of as *being saved* or *born again*. Our past sins are not only forgiven, but we are transformed to live a new life with God's power and grace. The New Testament makes it clear that this gift of salvation, becoming righteous, or exchanging identities comes by faith — not works — or any merit of our own (Ephesians 2:8).

✓ **4** How is true salvation a surrender and an exchange of identities between you and Jesus (Galatians 2:20)? What are the implications for you once you surrender the control of your life to Christ?

B) P115) A "HATRED OF SIN AND LOVE OF HOLINESS"

Transformation Is Inevitable

Now the Lord is the Spirit, and where the Spirit of the Lord is, there is freedom. And we, who with unveiled faces all reflect the Lord's glory, are being transformed into his likeness with ever-increasing glory, which comes from the Lord, who is the Spirit.

2 Corinthians 3:17–18

Therefore, if anyone is in Christ, he is a new creation; the old has gone, the new has come!

2 Corinthians 5:17

"Just what is saving faith?" is a good question for us to ask in today's culture, where everything is a subjective choice. "Making a decision for Christ" may be an unhelpfully vague description of what faith entails. Were we really repentant? Did we intend to cooperate with God in His work and our transformation? God alone knows the heart and whether our surrender at the cross and our commitment to the Lordship of Christ is genuine. In a sincere conversion, however, we will soon experience changing affections and habits. Things that used to seem appealing no longer do; things that weren't appealing now are. If your faith is alive, you will experience increasing discontent and conviction over sins of the past and will respond with a genuine desire to turn away, to be changed.

5 How is true Christianity more than a mere intellectual assent to the doctrines of the faith but a commitment to an ongoing process of transformation? Describe some ways that after receiving Jesus Christ into your life, God has begun over time to change your priorities, desires, and habits.

Saved to Do Good Works

For we are God's workmanship, created in Christ Jesus to do good works, which God prepared in advance for us to do.

Ephesians 2:10

People read Ephesians 2:8–9: "It is by grace you have been saved, through faith — and this not from yourselves, it is the gift of God — not by works, so that no one can boast." But they don't read the next verse (10): "For we are God's workmanship, created in Christ Jesus to do good works, which God prepared in advance for us to do." You've been saved in order to do good things. If you are a true Christian, your gratitude for what God has done for you on the cross and your gratitude for your sins being forgiven will compel you to do your duty as a Christian. You can't rest if you're not doing it. I find if I'm not doing what I think God's called me to do, I'm uncomfortable. And that's a holy discomfort.

/ **6** **(A)** Why does a life transformed by Jesus result in good works?
(B) If good works are the result of true salvation, what are the
<u>implications</u> for someone who professes faith but whose life and
behaviors remain largely unchanged? (See James 2:20.) On the other
hand, how might it be possible to do good works, and yet not be truly
saved? (See Ephesians 2:8–9.)

Ⓐ *ALOVE OF GOD LEADS TO A DESIRE TO PLEASE GOD.*

Ⓑ *THAT PERSON HAS NOT MADE THE LEAP. NO MATTER
WHAT HE SAYS*

Ⓒ *ONE CAN STILL BE A LOVING, GENEROUS,
AND MORAL PERSON WITHOUT FAITH. BUT SALVATION*
? *WILL ELUDE YOU.*

Costly Grace — Christian Suffering

> In this you greatly rejoice, though now for a little while you may have had
> to suffer grief in all kinds of trials. These have come so that your faith—of
> greater worth than gold, which perishes even though refined by fire—may be
> proved genuine and may result in praise, glory and honor when Jesus Christ is
> revealed. Though you have not seen him, you love him; and even though you
> do not see him now, you believe in him and are filled with an inexpressible
> and glorious joy, for you are receiving the goal of your faith, the salvation of
> your souls.
>
> 1 Peter 1:6–9

Sadly, in today's self-obsessed culture many see "being saved" as the
ticket to a nice, comfortable, blessed life. Period. But there's one thing
you can be sure of: you *will* be tested. New believers and mature believers alike need to understand, contrary to what popular books tell us, that
the Christian life is not without pain, difficulty, and suffering. When I
was released from prison after my highly publicized conversion, a number
of friends wanted to avoid me, confiding to others that they weren't as
concerned about associating with a former convict as a strange-talking

religious fanatic. You will soon discover this soft hostility in the workplace, perhaps at home, certainly in your social circles. More serious challenges will come about because of your newfound concern for others; you won't be able to ignore people's needs or injustice as you might have earlier. That's why so many contented middle-class folks I've known have, after coming to Christ, become involved in prison ministry or helping neighbors or volunteering at a hospice. This can be a joy, as I've discovered working among prisoners, but it can also exact a heavy price.

7 **If salvation is a free gift, why does it sometimes seem costly? What makes suffering joyous?**

Suffering Is Redeemed

And he said, "The Son of Man must suffer many things and be rejected by the elders, chief priests and teachers of the law, and he must be killed and on the third day be raised to life." Then he said to them all: "If anyone would come after me, he must deny himself and take up his cross daily and follow me. For whoever wants to save his life will lose it, but whoever loses his life for me will save it."

Luke 9:22–24

Suffering belongs to our calling as Christians. After their first arrest, the apostles left the Sanhedrin's court "rejoicing because they had been counted worthy of suffering disgrace for the Name" (Acts 5:41). It was a

privilege to share in His work. In many places today Christians are called
to suffer persecution for the sake of the Gospel. In India, North Korea,
Myanmar (Burma), and scores of other countries, Christians risk their lives
by even professing Christ—something most of us in the West know little
of. So the real question is not *whether* we will suffer but how we will react
to adversity *when it comes*. We can see it as a miserable experience to be
endured, or we can offer it to God for His redemptive purposes. This is the
great truth Christians know: God will always use what we suffer for Christ's
work of redemption if we let Him.

8 **In what ways does God grow us through our sufferings? Briefly
share a personal example, if time permits. How can we learn to
cooperate with God when faced with adversity?**

Suffering as a Witness

> For I was hungry and you gave me something to eat, I was thirsty and you
> gave me something to drink, I was a stranger and you invited me in, I needed
> clothes and you clothed me, I was sick and you looked after me, I was in
> prison and you came to visit me. . . . I tell you the truth, whatever you did for
> one of the least of these brothers of mine, you did for me.
>
> Matthew 25:35–36; 40

When the plague hit Rome in the third century, just as the church was flourishing, all the doctors and nurses fled, leaving people dying in the streets in agony. The Christians all stayed. They ministered to the dying. It was such an overpowering witness that when the plague receded and the people started returning to the city, everybody flocked to the Christian Church because they had been willing to sacrifice themselves in love of their neighbors. That's pure Christianity—suffering with those who are suffering—which is exactly what we're told to do.

9 **History is filled with examples of Christians giving themselves for others. How is the way a Christian <u>suffers in service</u> of others a powerful witness of the goodness of God to an unbelieving world? To <u>what extent</u> do you think Christians today are willing to genuinely suffer to advance the kingdom of Christ?**

WESTERN CIVILIZATION DOES NOT INSPIRE SACRIFICE. LOOK esp. TO EUROPE WHERE PEOPLE AREN'T EVEN WILLING TO HAVE CHILDREN. —

ARE WE IN A DECLINE?

Forgiveness and Reconciliation

All this is from God, who reconciled us to himself through Christ and gave us the ministry of reconciliation: that God was reconciling the world to himself in Christ, not counting men's sins against them. And he has committed to us the message of reconciliation.

2 Corinthians 5:18–19

At the cross Christ reaches out to us, reconciling us to God and calling us to be reconciled with one another. This invitation to reconciliation is universal, applying to all nations and all peoples, to rich and poor, bound and free. It's an unconditional invitation to each of us. Forgiveness, which makes reconciliation possible, is the centerpiece of the biblical account. When practiced, forgiveness is life-changing, even world-changing. And it often plays out in the most dramatic and unexpected ways.

No other religion has the same commandment that we ought to forgive others and love our enemies. It's the only belief system that provides for forgiveness and reconciliation—and brings people together. The problem in the Middle East today is a result of Islam having no concept of forgiveness, which is why the battling sects of Islam can never reconcile. We as Christians are given this great gift, the ministry of reconciliation (2 Corinthians 5:18). The first step, if Christians are to be faithful ministers of reconciliation, is to repent of our own failures and to practice this consistently.

√ **10** Read the summary of Bible verses in the following chart. Why are these examples of forgiveness and reconciliation so central to the heart of God? In which of these areas is God leading you to take a step of faith?

2 Corinthians 5:17–19	God has given his followers the ministry of reconciliation.
Matthew 5:44	Jesus commands us to love and pray for our enemies.
Matthew 6:12	We are to forgive our debtors.
Romans 12:17	We are not to repay anyone evil with evil.
Romans 12:20	If our enemies are hungry, we are to feed them.
Romans 12:21	We are not to overcome evil with evil, but with good.

The Scandal of Division

My prayer is not for them alone. I pray also for those who will believe in me through their message, that all of them may be one, Father, just as you are in me and I am in you. May they also be in us so that the world may believe that you have sent me. I have given them the glory that you gave me, that they may be one as we are one: I in them and you in me. May they be brought to complete unity to let the world know that you sent me and have loved them even as you have loved me.

John 17:20–23

If forgiveness and reconciliation are at the heart of the Gospel, if Christ can reconcile murderers with their victims' loved ones and even bring about peaceful settlements of religious wars, what then do we say about division among true Christians? We must repent of it. The scandal to the world must be the cross, not our division. In a world where Christianity is being assaulted on all sides, true believers must stand together in common defense of the faith. It is the challenge of the Church to work toward this, imperfect though our efforts may be, as we profess one Lord, one faith, and one baptism.

11 **If Jesus models, teaches, and commands us to pray for forgiveness, reconciliation, and unity, why is the Church still so divided—and to what detriment?**

Unity — Across the Confessional Divide

Be completely humble and gentle; be patient, bearing with one another in love. Make every effort to keep the unity of the Spirit through the bond of peace. There is one body and one Spirit — just as you were called to one hope when you were called — one Lord, one faith, one baptism; one God and Father of all, who is over all and through all and in all.

Ephesians 4:2 – 6

A new command I give you: Love one another. As I have loved you, so you must love one another. By this all men will know that you are my disciples, if you love one another.

John 13:34 – 35

Christians must see across the confessional divides — the valleys that keep denominations separate, and keep Protestants and Catholics apart — and seek unity within the body of Christ. In the seventeenth century, a Puritan pastor, Richard Baxter, believed that there was a "core of orthodox Christianity that Puritans, Anglicans, and Catholics could all affirm … that should have been a source of peace among them." Baxter's argument remains in our time the greatest hope for at least the partial fulfillment of Christ's prayers for unity.

This was on Jesus' heart the night before He was crucified when He prayed for all who would believe "that all of them may be one, Father, just as you are in me, and I am in you. May they also be in us so that the world may believe that you have sent me" (John 17:21). In the midst of his passion and suffering, knowing that He was to go to the cross the next morning, these were His very last pleas to the Father. In the light of these Scriptures, can a true Christian ever seek to perpetuate disunity?

12 **How can the universal Church begin to heal divisions without compromising a commitment to orthodox truth? How might *you* begin to build bridges of Christian fellowship and unity?**

DVD Closing Segment and Prayer (5 minutes)

Use the space provided below to take notes on anything that stands out to you.

Before the Next Session

Choose one or more of the following ways to further digest and apply the concepts and principles you're learning:

• **Set aside some alone time to prayerfully reflect and meditate on the material covered in this session.** You might wish to review all of the summary sections preceding each question, or select the particular Scripture verses and corresponding synopsis you feel God is leading you to study. As you meditate and focus on God's Word, let his truth fill you. And as you pray and invite the Holy Spirit to transform and renew your mind, consider what God may be teaching you. What new insights have you discovered; what fresh perspectives have you gained; how might you apply these things to your everyday life? Use the space below to journal these things.

- **Meet with one or two other people from your group to further discuss how you might apply what you're learning to your everyday life.** Share with one another what has impacted you and how God is especially speaking to you. Discuss what concepts or topics have been particularly difficult for you to understand or accept. Also be sure to set aside some time to pray together.

- **Initiate a dialogue with someone who is not a participant in your group.** Invite a friend who is not yet a Christian to interact with you over some of the concepts you have been covering in the book, DVD clips, and group discussion. Be especially careful to listen with a sincere desire to hear and understand what your friend believes and why. Ask your friend if he or she would be interested in hearing some of the ways you've been impacted by your study of the material. You may wish to share some of the insights you gained from your conversation with the rest of your group when you meet again.

Also, in preparation for session four, please read chapter 7 of the book *The Faith*.

THE TRINITY — GOD ABOVE, GOD BESIDE, GOD WITHIN

God is all powerful, all knowing, the ultimate source of all reality. Serious Christians must understand the nature of this God in His fullness, particularly God's Trinitarian nature and God's sovereignty. Both are crucial to the freedom of the Christian life.

Charles Colson

Before You Begin

This session is planned for 50 minutes, including two DVD segments and 12 discussion questions (some of which also include follow-up questions). If time is a constraint, feel free to select only those questions most pertinent to your group discussion.

The synopsis preceding each question or questions is designed to provide a short summary of the content covered by that question or questions. During your group time, we encourage you to read the Scripture(s) together. While it is not necessary to read the summaries during the meeting, your group will be better prepared to take the discussion to a deeper level if you are able to read and meditate on them in advance.

Make every effort to read chapter 7 of the book *The Faith* prior to the session. This corresponding chapter provides a more in-depth explanation of the concepts addressed in this session's DVD segments, the summary sections, and the group discussion questions that follow.

DVD Teaching Segment (20 minutes)

Notes

The nature of God

Explaining the Trinity

Understanding the Trinity—a constant love relationship

Saving grace and common grace

God created time itself

DVD Group Discussion (25 minutes)

Defending the Trinity

> *Dear friends, do not believe every spirit, but test the spirits to see whether they are from God, because many false prophets have gone out into the world. This is how you can recognize the Spirit of God: Every spirit that acknowledges that Jesus Christ has come in the flesh is from God, but every spirit that does not acknowledge Jesus is not from God. This is the spirit of the antichrist, which you have heard is coming and even now is already in the world. You, dear children, are from God and have overcome them, because the one who is in you is greater than the one who is in the world. They are from the world and therefore speak from the viewpoint of the world, and the world listens to them.*
>
> 1 John 4:1–5

The Trinity—Father, Son, and Holy Spirit, one God in three persons—is often considered to be mysterious at best, self-contradicting at worst. Everyone would acknowledge that the idea of a triune God—three in one—is the most difficult of all Christian doctrines, which is why so many neglect it or even write it off. But this is tragic. As St. Caesarius of Arles said in the sixth century, "The faith of all Christians rests on the Trinity." While the Trinity transcends the bounds of human understanding, this doctrine is at the heart of Christian spirituality, and in the life of faith we experience its truth at every turn. Understanding the doctrine of the Trinity is especially timely in today's titanic clash of civilizations when, for example, some Muslim activists contend that the Trinity is a form of idolatry and that Christianity is a form of polytheism—the worship of more than one God—in disguise.

1 **What are some ways you have heard the Trinity explained? How would you begin to explain or defend the three-in-one nature of the Christian God to someone of another religion?**

God is what we seek, that person above & beyond us.

Jesus is that real person beside us, asisting us with our journey with his words,

The Holy Spirit is God within that nudges us to seek Him.

2 What are the advantages for Christians to be able to explain or defend the concept of the Trinity? What are the potential consequences for those who cannot?

IF ONE GRAPPLES WITH, AND ULTIMATELY UNDERSTANDS THE TRINITY ONE UNDERSTANDS THE UNIVERSALITY OF GOD. IN THE TRINITY WE SEE THAT GOD IS EVERYWHERE IN THE UNIVERSE, ABOVE, BESIDE, & WITHIN US.

The Trinity — God Above, God Beside, God Within

Then Jesus came to them and said, "All authority in heaven and on earth has been given to me. Therefore go and make disciples of all nations, baptizing them in the name of the Father and of the Son and of the Holy Spirit, and teaching them to obey everything I have commanded you. And surely I am with you always, to the very end of the age."

Matthew 28:18–20

Our experience of the Trinity is actually a common part of everyday Christian experience. We invoke the Trinity every time we recite the Lord's Prayer. Our heavenly Father supplies our daily bread; through Jesus Christ the Father forgives our sins; and by the power of the Holy Spirit we can overcome temptation.

The biblical revelation discloses the Trinitarian nature of God in a long-prepared historical sequence: God the Creator in Genesis, Jesus the Son at the beginning of the New Testament, and the Holy Spirit in Pentecost's confirming of the Church. The New Testament is clearly Trinitarian in its witness. Jesus' great commission to His followers to make disciples of all nations includes the instruction, "baptizing them *in the name of the Father and of the Son and of the Holy Spirit*" (Matthew 28:19, emphasis added). So, he introduces the Trinity in the context of baptism, right there, and tells us to baptize in the name of all three.

3 Using the chart below, further unpack and distinguish the roles of the three persons of the Trinity. How adequately does the doctrine of the Trinity fully represent the nature of God? Explain.

God as Creator, or God Above	*Genesis 1:1–3, 26; John 1:1–5* LIFE, LIGHT, ALL THINGS
God as Redeemer, or God Beside	*John 19–21; John 10:30; 14:6–9* I the the know me
God as Sustainer, or God Within	*John 14:15–18; 16:3; Acts 1:7–8; 2:1–21* SPIRIT WITHIN YOU

THE TRINITY PRETTY MUCH COVERS IT!

THERE IS NO ESCAPING, GOD IS EVERYWHERE IN THE WORLD WHICH HE CREATED. HE IS ALSO EVERYWHERE ON A PERSONAL BASIS — ABOVE, BESIDE, WITHIN.

4 Why do you think Jesus made a point to include all three Persons of the Trinity in his final commission to believers? How is each member of the Trinity integral to the mission of the Church?

The Triune God Is Love

> *Dear friends, since God so loved us, we also ought to love one another.*
> *No one has ever seen God; but if we love one another, God lives in us and*
> *his love is made complete in us. We know that we live in him and he in us,*
> *because he has given us of his Spirit. And we have seen and testify that the*
> *Father has sent his Son to be the Savior of the world. If anyone acknowledges*
> *that Jesus is the Son of God, God lives in him and he in God. And so we*
> *know and rely on the love God has for us. God is love. Whoever lives in love*
> *lives in God, and God in him.*
>
> 1 John 4:11 – 16

The Trinity enables us to better understand the scriptural teaching that God is love. Love cannot exist without someone to love, which is why Allah, and any unitary understanding, leads to a cold, impersonal god. The essence of the God of the Bible is His intertwined triune nature of Father, Son, and Holy Spirit. The three continuously pour out love to one another and receive love in return. The Trinity exists as a perfect community of self-giving. In this life, Christians enjoy participation in this community through the indwelling of the Holy Spirit, and in the world to come we will be united with the Godhead in perfect love. The Trinity sums up our final hope. What could be more central to our faith?

5 Explain how God was the embodiment of love before he created anything or anyone, and how the Trinity gives us a more meaningful picture of this truth.

6 How does the triune nature of the Christian God offer an intimate and personal relationship with him in ways that the gods of other belief systems do not?

The Trinity includes a person in Jesus which gives the simple human mind a God we can love. It is not possible to have a personal relationship with Allah. Sure, Allah Akbar, God is Great is a true statement but it falls far short of the Trinity which brings God into & beside us..

The Triune God Is Sovereign

In the beginning God created the heavens and the earth. Now the earth was formless and empty, darkness was over the surface of the deep, and the Spirit of God was hovering over the waters. . . . Then God said, "Let us make man in our image, in our likeness, and let them rule over the fish of the sea and the birds of the air, over the livestock, over all the earth, and over all the creatures that move along the ground."

Genesis 1:1–2, 26

For by [Jesus] all things were created: things in heaven and on earth, visible and invisible, whether thrones or powers or rulers or authorities; all things were created by him and for him. He is before all things, and in him all things hold together.

Colossians 1:16–17

Note that all three persons of the Trinity play key roles in creating and sustaining the world. The Father speaks the world into existence through His Word, which is carried out by the Holy Spirit. We glimpse the Holy Spirit in the creation account brooding like a dove over the waters of the unformed abyss. The apostle Paul pays particular attention to how Christ sustains the world (see Colossians 1:16–17 above). The phrase "all things hold together" in Christ is striking. He is essentially the glue of the universe, the binding force of the created order. Scholars like John Polkinghorne, a noted physicist and former president of Queens College,

Cambridge, now an Anglican priest, argue that Christ is the animating force that keeps the universe in order and existence. Think about it this way: He is the information—the *Logos*—behind all the carriers of information like DNA. This gives new meaning to God's rule, God's power, and God's understanding—all of which are infinite. God's sovereignty over all of creation cannot be denied.

7 **What does it mean to say that God is sovereign over all creation? If this is so, how and why does Satan still continue to occupy and intervene in this world?**

God created, is responsible for life light, etc
+ is about, beside, + within us.

Free will? Is part of the plan...

A Christian View of Time

> But do not forget this one thing, dear friends: With the Lord a day is like a
> thousand years, and a thousand years are like a day. The Lord is not slow in
> keeping his promise, as some understand slowness. He is patient with you,
> not wanting anyone to perish, but everyone to come to repentance.
>
> 2 Peter 3:8–9

Time is not a commodity as we're accustomed to thinking of it. Time is the most precious thing we have because it's the relationship with God that we live for moment by moment. No time is insignificant; what you do today counts forever.

How does this doctrine, unique to the Christian worldview, affect us? Why does it matter? Once you see the triune God as dwelling apart from time and space, in what we can only imagine as an eternal present, God's liberation from every circumstance, even the losses of time, acquires rich new meaning. We live in an entirely new way. For good reason the Scriptures celebrate the "glorious freedom of the children of God" (Romans 8:21).

8 How does one's view of time impact the way one lives? Christians believe that since God created everything, including time itself, people will one day exist outside of time! How does a Christian worldview of time differ from a secular worldview of time? How does a Christian view of time change the way *you* live today?

The Cultural Commission

The LORD God took the man and put him in the Garden of Eden to work it and take care of it. . . . Now the LORD God had formed out of the ground all the beasts of the field and all the birds of the air. He brought them to the man to see what he would name them; and whatever the man called each living creature, that was its name.

Genesis 2:15, 19

You are the salt of the earth. But if the salt loses its saltiness, how can it be made salty again? It is no longer good for anything, except to be thrown out and trampled by men. You are the light of the world. A city on a hill cannot be hidden.

Matthew 5:13 – 14

There are two kinds of grace: saving grace and common grace. Saving grace is that which works for our salvation. Common grace is the good we do that holds back the flood of sin and evil that would otherwise overturn the world. God enables us to do acts of common grace so that we're doing it for the greater good of all people.

Christianity is a way of seeing all of life, every aspect of reality; it is a worldview. This means that we have two divinely authorized commissions. The first is well known—the Great Commission: to make disciples and baptize them (Matthew 28:19). But the second is equally important. It is to bring the righteousness of God to bear on all of life, to take dominion, to carry out the tasks we are given in the first chapters of Genesis, to bring a redeeming influence into a fallen culture. This is our Cultural Commission.

9 **What is the Cultural Commission and how is it supported in Scripture? In what specific ways can you implement this mandate to bring God's justice and righteousness within your sphere of influence?**

10 **What are some examples of Christians or Christian movements that have taken the Cultural Commission seriously and extended common grace in such a way as to restrain the flood of sin and evil?**

Christianity Is Rational and Reasonable

In the beginning was the Word, and the Word was with God, and the Word was God. He was with God in the beginning. Through him all things were made; without him nothing was made that has been made.

John 1:1–3

Christians believe that the most likely explanation for a reasonable universe and one in which we experience ourselves as free can be found in a reasonable, personal God. Greek philosophy embraced the concept of *logos*, an ultimate creative reason as the source of all things. The Gospel of John applies this concept to Christ, as the *Logos* or Word of God through whom all things came to be (John 1:1–3). Christians see the creation as an indicator of God's character. When we look at nature, we are immediately impressed by its creativity and beauty. Christians wonder why beauty should exist in such abundance if the creative reason did not mean to communicate love.

Only a creative reason, or *Logos*, does justice to our experience of the world. Further, only a *Logos* that is both unimaginably creative and loving accounts for our delight in the world. When we see the *Logos* as the source of creation and yet independent of it, when we reflect on the world's beauty and our own freedom, the *Logos* quickly assumes the character of the personal God described in the Scriptures.

11 **Because Jesus is the Word (what the Greeks called "logos") — the ultimate creative reason and source of all things — what does the order and beauty of the world he created tell us about the nature and character of God?**

GIVING, LOVING, GENEROUS BEING!

12 How do the tangible benefits of Christianity lend themselves to a reasonable and rational belief in God? In what ways has your faith been reinforced by your Christian experience?

DVD Closing Segment and Prayer (5 minutes)

Use the space provided below to take notes on anything that stands out to you.

Before the Next Session

Choose one or more of the following ways to further digest and apply the concepts and principles you're learning:

• **Set aside some alone time to prayerfully reflect and meditate on the material covered in this session.** You might wish to review all of the summary sections preceding each question, or select the particular Scripture verses and corresponding synopsis you feel God is leading you to study. As you meditate and focus on God's Word, let his truth fill you. And as you pray and invite the Holy Spirit to transform and renew your mind, consider what God may be teaching you. What new insights have you discovered; what fresh perspectives have you gained; how might you apply these things to your everyday life? Use the space below to journal these things.

- **Meet with one or two other people from your group to further discuss how you might apply what you're learning to your everyday life.** Share with one another what has impacted you and how God is especially speaking to you. Discuss what concepts or topics have been particularly difficult for you to understand or accept. Also be sure to set aside some time to pray together.

- **Initiate a dialogue with someone who is not a participant in your group.** Invite a friend who is not yet a Christian to interact with you over some of the concepts you have been covering in the book, DVD clips, and group discussion. Be especially careful to listen with a sincere desire to hear and understand what your friend believes and why. Ask your friend if he or she would be interested in hearing some of the ways you've been impacted by your study of the material. You may wish to share some of the insights you gained from your conversation with the rest of your group when you meet again.

Also, in preparation for session five, please read chapters 10–12 of the book *The Faith*.

BE HOLY —
TRANSFORM
THE WORLD!

Where these marks are present — the preaching of the Word, the administration of the sacraments, the exercise of discipline, and the practice of community — the Church will inevitably transform the culture around it. . . . When we are the Church as Christ commands us to be, we change and so does the world.

Charles Colson

Before You Begin

This session is planned for 50 minutes, including two DVD segments and 12 discussion questions (some of which also include follow-up questions). If time is a constraint, feel free to select only those questions most pertinent to your group discussion.

The synopsis preceding each question or questions is designed to provide a short summary of the content covered by that question or questions. During your group time, we encourage you to read the Scripture(s) together. While it is not necessary to read the summaries during the meeting, your group will be better prepared to take the discussion to a deeper level if you are able to read and meditate on them in advance.

Make every effort to read chapters 10–12 of the book *The Faith* prior to the session. These corresponding chapters provide a more in-depth explanation of the concepts addressed in this session's DVD segments, the summary sections, and the group discussion questions that follow.

DVD Teaching Segment (20 minutes)

Notes

Two definitions of the Church

The sacraments (or ordinances) of the Church

The purpose of the Church

Holiness: Completely consecrated to God

Caring about justice, righteousness, and society: Pro-life at every stage

DVD Group Discussion (25 minutes)

The Church

When the people heard this, they were cut to the heart and said to Peter and the other apostles, "Brothers, what shall we do?" Peter replied, "Repent and be baptized, every one of you, in the name of Jesus Christ for the forgiveness of your sins. And you will receive the gift of the Holy Spirit. . . . They devoted themselves to the apostles' teaching and to the fellowship, to the breaking of bread and to prayer.

Acts 2:37 – 38, 42

On the cross, Christ not only reconciles us to Himself but incorporates us into His body, the Church, which consists of all those who have accepted Christ's offer of salvation — what the early Church called the *communio sanctorum*, the community of saints. As individual Christians, we are also called to be part of a specific confessing body, or local church, where our spiritual duties and disciplines can be fulfilled. This is the community God had in mind before time itself began. We cannot understand the Church without seeing her as part of the sweeping story the Bible tells, and we cannot be faithful Christians without affirming God's central role for the Church — the living body of Christ. The Church is a reclamation project, reestablishing God's rule in the midst of a world still mostly under Satan's sway. This is much different in character and purpose from the common perception.

Another function of the Church is the administration of the sacraments. A sacrament is simply a mark to the world of the presence of God — an outward sign of an inward and spiritual reality. Every church practices at least two sacraments, although some call them ordinances. The first is the Lord's Supper, the Eucharist, when we share the body and blood of Christ. The second sacrament, or ordinance, is baptism. This sacrament reveals for all that we have been buried with Christ and resurrected to walk in the newness of life. It is the sign that we are united with Him and now part of His body.

1 Contrast the common perception of the Church with the character and purpose of the Church given in Scripture. When does one become a part of the Church, and what is the distinction between membership in God's universal Church and membership in a local church?

Church is a communia of Savis

Church not because we get God stuff from it but because it is a place to love God.

'The Church glorifies God + is our vehicle to participate in God's life (p 14)

Genuine Community

All the believers were one in heart and mind. No one claimed that any of his possessions was his own, but they shared everything they had. With great power the apostles continued to testify to the resurrection of the Lord Jesus, and much grace was upon them all. There were no needy persons among them. For from time to time those who owned lands or houses sold them, brought the money from the sales and put it at the apostles' feet, and it was distributed to anyone as he had need.

Acts 4:32–35

Genuine community also characterizes the Church. The apostle Paul reminds the church in Rome, "In Christ we who are many form one body, and each member belongs to all the others" (Romans 12:5). How we belong to one another goes far beyond the "sweet fellowship" of potluck suppers and finding a comfortable social circle. True community involves a real *koinonia*, a deep communion—the kind the apostles described in Acts 4, which is the first real sign of the Kingdom on earth, where each person in need was helped. This is where people truly bear one another's burdens, pray for one another, and yes, even suffer for one another.

2 What are some of the distinguishing characteristics of genuine Christian community? What changes could you make in your own life that would encourage or support this kind of communion in your own church?

Worship

> *Then I looked and heard the voice of many angels, numbering thousands upon thousands, and ten thousand times ten thousand. They encircled the throne and the living creatures and the elders. In a loud voice they sang: "Worthy is the Lamb, who was slain, to receive power and wealth and wisdom and strength and honor and glory and praise!" Then I heard every creature in heaven and on earth and under the earth and on the sea, and all that is in them, singing: "To him who sits on the throne and to the Lamb be praise and honor and glory and power, for ever and ever!"*
>
> Revelation 5:11 – 13

The Church is the gathering of saints and angels in holy festival which takes place even on earth as we enter into worship. We worship God because God is worthy of our worship. The Church glorifies God on earth, and this is a primary means by which we participate in God's life. When Jesus said the gates of hell cannot stand against His Church, He was foreseeing the people of God, drawn into unity with God and each other through worship, spilling out of our meeting places to spread the Gospel and righteousness. How else could we assault the gates of hell? You won't confront most of the world's darkness in your comfortable sanctuary. Have we forgotten this? We worship God in our churches so we can follow Him in the world.

3 What does it mean to worship God, and why do we do it? How do you worship God outside of the church building and in your everyday life?

To worship God is to love God. We express this love by leading a life which pleases Him. This includes going to Church, leading a life obeying His rules, listening to Him through prayer.

Evangelism

> *"But you will receive power when the Holy Spirit comes on you; and you will be my witnesses in Jerusalem, and in all Judea and Samaria, and to the ends of the earth."*
>
> Acts 1:8

The Church exists not only as a worshiping community but also as a missionary community. Evangelism always has to be a primary call in the Church. The truth is that the Gospel should be radiating out from our churches, the messages in the pulpit translated by those in the pew. We often think that evangelism belongs mainly to the clergy, but every church member has a particular ability and calling to extend the Church's witness into the world. Not everyone is going to come into a church. As I have discovered, often the most effective way in which a church can evangelize is to seek out opportunities for its members to share the Gospel through informal discussion groups in the workplace, in homes, and in community halls, and draw people in however we can reach them.

4 Why is it important for Christians to share their faith outside the walls of the church? What are some effective, practical ways of doing that?

Personal Holiness

But you are a chosen people, a royal priesthood, a holy nation, a people belonging to God, that you may declare the praises of him who called you out of darkness into his wonderful light.

1 Peter 2:9

I am the LORD who brought you up out of Egypt to be your God; therefore be holy, because I am holy.

Leviticus 11:45

Most nonbelievers, and many Christians, confuse holiness with following a legalistic list of do's-and-don'ts or reduce it to piety and attentiveness to religious duties. In reality, holiness embraces piety, but it is much more; it is the heart of the Christian life and every Christian's destiny. As one devotional writer put it, God has one eternal purpose for us, that we should be "conformed to the likeness of his Son" (Romans 8:29). We are to become holy as Christ is holy; we are to become true Christians, the root meaning of which is "little Christs."

5 How is the pursuit of holiness different from attempting to follow a prescribed list of do's and don'ts? What is the role of the local church with regard to challenging and supporting believers in the pursuit of personal holiness? What is your role?

Holiness is, at its best, to be like Christ. A list of do's & don'ts does not require a change of one's heart. Actions or non actions do not require a love of God or of neighbor.

The local church can present & explain scripture, can give opportunities to treat others well, can promote censure behavior.

My role is to be as holy as possible as a mirror to others & to encourage & support holiness in others.

Social Holiness

> Make every effort to live in peace with all men and to be holy; without holiness no one will see the Lord. See to it that no one misses the grace of God and that no bitter root grows up to cause trouble and defile many.
>
> Hebrews 12:14 – 15

Holiness doesn't stop with our own condition but carries over into actions that affect the world around us. John Wesley famously said there is no holiness apart from social holiness. Many young evangelicals, including those in the emerging-church movement, are echoing this call, and they are right to do so. It's not enough to be comfortable in our gathering places of worship. When we care for God's favorites, the poor, who include the destitute, the widowed, the fatherless, the sick, prisoners, and anyone suffering injustice, we plunge immediately into the cosmic battle that's always raging between good and evil. We choose sides. We discern the things we see in the culture around us, and explode the false myths that we are urged to live by.

6 What are some of the false myths within our culture that we are urged to live by? How might we begin to explode these myths in our day-to-day lives?

In Defense of Human Rights

Wash and make yourselves clean. Take your evil deeds out of my sight! Stop doing wrong, learn to do right! Seek justice, encourage the oppressed. Defend the cause of the fatherless, plead the case of the widow.

Isaiah 1:16–17

When you look at the history of Christian awakenings and movements, you find one common denominator running through all of them. They did what they did not because it was some noble cause for society or because they believed in some social gospel or because they wanted political influence. They acted because they believed, as God's holy people, that they were called both to end systemic evil *and* reform cultural attitudes.

7 How important is it for Christians and the Church to take a stand against unjust laws? How can individual Christians possibly contribute to ending systemic evils and reforming cultural attitudes?

BIG QUESTION!

VOTE, STANDUP, SUPPORT JUST ORGANIZATIONS

MAKING YOUR OPINION KNOWN, EOS WHEN THAT OPINION IS UNPOPULAR IS A SMALL BUT IMPORTANT STEP.

The Christian View of Humanity

*So God created man in his own image, in the image of God he created him;
male and female he created them.*

Genesis 1:27

Christians believe that men and women were created intentionally and purposefully in God's image. All serious Christians take issue with the secular view that humanity has no specific purpose; that creation is unintentional and random. The argument for design is clear in Scripture, which records that the "heavens declare the glory of God" (Psalm 19:1) — in other words, God has left His imprint on creation. Created by God and with His purpose for us clear, human life is sacred.

This is, in fact, the preeminent form the battle of good versus evil has taken in our day — as it did in the early days of the Church. This may sound inflammatory and extreme to some, but what could be more crucial than whether the worth of a life comes from being created in the image of God or from its usefulness to society?

8 Why is the desire to play God with human life (by engineering for designer babies, cloning organs, and destroying embryos for research) an example of the worst in human nature? When carried out to its logical conclusion, and without a biblically based set of ethics, where does this secular worldview end?

The Secular View of Humanity

For it is written: "I will destroy the wisdom of the wise; the intelligence of the intelligent I will frustrate." Where is the wise man? Where is the scholar? Where is the philosopher of this age? Has not God made foolish the wisdom of the world?

1 Corinthians 1:19–20

The secular view of humanity excludes the idea of an inherent purpose. Secularists emphasize the continuity of the evolutionary process, seeing humanity as just another example of evolution's chance handiwork, no different in kind than lice and lungfish. Since the universe came about for unknown reasons and life evolved by chance, humanity must invent its own reasons for being and the ethics by which we will govern ourselves. That means whose lives we value becomes a matter of choice.

The secularist may genuinely believe that he loves his neighbor, but in the end he may love him so much that he decides to put him out of his misery. Without a biblically based set of ethics rooted in the sanctity of life, without the established natural order clearly expressed in law and practice, we are left to the tender mercies of those in authority. And we embrace that at our certain peril.

9 **A Christian worldview teaches that a state or government alone can never ensure an idyllic society. Explain why not.**

"No OBJECTIVE BASIS FOR DETERMINING HUMAN NATURE"

FOUNDING FATHERS OF US DID A GOOD JOB WITH LIFE LIBERTY, PURSUIT OF HAPPINESS. BUT MUCH OF THE SUCCESS OF THIS AMMERICAN REPUBLIC AROUND RECOGNITION OF GOD & THE VALUE OF THE INDIVIDUAL.

THESE PRINCIPLES CAN BE HEAVEN ON EARTH IN A HOLY INDIVIDUAL BUT MAN IN THE AGGREGATE IS A FALLEN CREATURE, UTOPIA IS BEYOND OUR HUMAN REACH.

The Sanctity of Human Life

See to it that no one takes you captive through hollow and deceptive philosophy, which depends on human tradition and the basic principles of this world rather than on Christ.

Colossians 2:8

When Christians today see life through God's eyes, just as William Wilberforce and his spiritual heirs did in the nineteenth century, we are compelled not only to care for the poor and vulnerable but to defend every human's God-given right. This is why Christians believe in the sanctity of life at every stage, from conception to death. In the Catholic view, the sanctity of human life is considered part of the Gospel itself; among evangelicals it is considered integral to the Gospel. This is why Evangelicals and Catholics Together, in perhaps its finest document, argues that "Christians who support the legal license to kill the innocent [must] consider whether they have not set themselves against the will of God and, to that extent, separated themselves from the company of Christian discipleship." That is a tough statement, but this issue separates true Christians from those who are simply along for the ride.

10 In what ways are Christians today conforming to a culture which supports the legal license to kill the innocent unborn? To what extent does defending life from conception to death reflect one's commitment to Christ? Explain.

The Defense of Human Life

For you created my inmost being; you knit me together in my mother's womb. I praise you because I am fearfully and wonderfully made; your works are wonderful, I know that full well. My frame was not hidden from you when I was made in the secret place. When I was woven together in the depths of the earth, your eyes saw my unformed body. All the days ordained for me were written in your book before one of them came to be.

Psalm 139:13 – 16

I tell you the truth, whatever you did not do for one of the least of these, you did not do for me.

Matthew 25:45

The Church's passionate engagement in politics in defense of life is not due to the emergence of the "big bad religious right," as Christianity's detractors might say (and many Christians mistakenly believe as well). It was the early Church that consistently challenged the state, describing abortion and infanticide in terms that would be politically incorrect today. The Church's defense of life unexpectedly turned out to be hugely popular in an ancient world where lions tearing people apart constituted entertainment. "Perhaps above all else," author Rodney Stark writes, "Christianity brought a new conception of humanity to a world saturated with capricious cruelty and the vicarious love of death."

But people still dispute *which* human beings, whatever their developmental state, possess the right to life. This was certainly not a difficult question for our Founding Fathers, whose moral views were shaped by biblical revelation. They wrote, "We hold these truths to be self-evident, that all men are created equal and endowed by their Creator with certain unalienable rights, among these are *life*, liberty and the pursuit of happiness."

11 **If every human life is created by God, in the image of God, how valuable is human life at the moment of conception? What obligation do Christians have to do whatever is within their power to defend, rescue, and deliver "the least of these"? Do you believe unborn human beings fall into this category?**

Propose, Educate, and Persuade

Blessed are those who are persecuted because of righteousness, for theirs is the kingdom of heaven. Blessed are you when people insult you, persecute you and falsely say all kinds of evil against you because of me. Rejoice and be glad, because great is your reward in heaven, for in the same way they persecuted the prophets who were before you.

Matthew 5:10–12

Conservative Christians are seen as concerned only with personal morality, ignoring issues such as social justice, the welfare of the poor, and human rights. And daily we hear the hue and cry about conservatives wanting to "impose" their views on an unwilling society. Interestingly, that fearsome phrase originated with the 1860 political campaign when Abraham Lincoln's opponents charged he was trying to "impose" his will upon slaveholders. We can be grateful he did and freed the slaveholders as well as the slaves from a morally corrupt and corrupting institution.

The simple fact is no one has the right in a free society to impose his will on anyone. All any citizen can do is contend for his point of view in the democratic process. So Christians do not impose; they *propose* a vision of a culture of life, to educate and *persuade*.

12 **Given the divided political landscape today, should Christians (and the Church) increase, continue, or cease addressing divisive issues such as abortion, marriage, and sexual morality? How might the Church more effectively address these issues? How might you?**

DVD Closing Segment and Prayer (5 minutes)

Use the space provided below to take notes on anything that stands out to you.

Before the Next Session

Choose one or more of the following ways to further digest and apply the concepts and principles you're learning:

- **Set aside some alone time to prayerfully reflect and meditate on the material covered in this session.** You might wish to review all of the summary sections preceding each question, or select the particular Scripture verses and corresponding synopsis you feel God is leading you to study. As you meditate and focus on God's Word, let his truth fill you. And as you pray and invite the Holy Spirit to transform and renew your mind, consider what God may be teaching you. What new insights have you discovered; what fresh perspectives have you gained; how might you apply these things to your everyday life? Use the space below to journal these things.

• **Meet with one or two other people from your group to further discuss how you might apply what you're learning to your everyday life.** Share with one another what has impacted you and how God is especially speaking to you. Discuss what concepts or topics have been particularly difficult for you to understand or accept. Also be sure to set aside some time to pray together.

• **Initiate a dialogue with someone who is not a participant in your group.** Invite a friend who is not yet a Christian to interact with you over some of the concepts you have been covering in the book, DVD clips, and group discussion. Be especially careful to listen with a sincere desire to hear and understand what your friend believes and why. Ask your friend if he or she would be interested in hearing some of the ways you've been impacted by your study of the material. You may wish to share some of the insights you gained from your conversation with the rest of your group when you meet again.

Also, in preparation for session six, please read chapters 13 – 15 of the book *The Faith*.

THE GREAT PROPOSAL

And can the liberties of a nation be thought secure when we have removed their only firm basis, a conviction in the minds of the people that these liberties are the gift of God? That they are not to be violated but with His wrath? Indeed I tremble for my country when I reflect that God is just; that His justice cannot sleep forever.

Thomas Jefferson

Before You Begin

This session is planned for 50 minutes, including two DVD segments and 12 discussion questions (some of which also include follow-up questions). If time is a constraint, feel free to select only those questions most pertinent to your group discussion.

The synopsis preceding each question or questions is designed to provide a short summary of the content covered by that question or questions. During your group time, we encourage you to read the Scripture(s) together. While it is not necessary to read the summaries during the meeting, your group will be better prepared to take the discussion to a deeper level if you are able to read and meditate on them in advance.

Make every effort to read chapters 13–15 of the book *The Faith* prior to the session. These corresponding chapters provide a more in-depth explanation of the concepts addressed in this session's DVD segments, the summary sections, and the group discussion questions that follow.

DVD Teaching Segment (20 minutes)

Notes

An innate sense of justice

The end of history will be Christ's return

The Christian life is the most joyful way to live (the joy of orthodoxy)

Historical markers of Christianity

Fighting for survival on two fronts

DVD Group Discussion (25 minutes)

An Innate Sense of Justice

> *Then men will say, "Surely the righteous still are rewarded; surely there is a God who judges the earth."*
>
> Psalm 58:11

All of us share a deeply ingrained sense that the scales must be balanced, that wrongs must somehow be righted. Christians believe this sense of justice arises from being made in God's image. As creatures of a just and loving Creator we long to see His character reflected in the world about us, if not always in our own actions. The moral law is written on our hearts (Romans 2:15). We cry out for the demands of justice to be satisfied, and we even sense that they will be someday. Many consider this hunger for justice persuasive evidence of God's existence and His final balancing of accounts in the afterlife. If the world were truly a random place, guided by no design or purpose, why would believers and nonbelievers alike have this sense of justice and look forward to its realization, in this life and eternity as well? This is why nearly every religion has embraced some form of judgment in the afterlife. Christianity confirms that our longing for the wicked to be punished and the good rewarded will be fulfilled on judgment day.

1 **Do you hold out hope that someday God will make all things right by judging good and evil? On what do you base this hope? How is our innate sense of justice a sign of God's existence?**

An Innate Sense of Eternal Love

> *Dear friends, let us love one another, for love comes from God. Everyone*
> *who loves has been born of God and knows God. Whoever does not love does*
> *not know God, because God is love.*
>
> 1 John 4:7–8

Love always envisions a limitless future. Saying "I will love you *forever*"
comes as naturally to lovers as breathing. But what happens if you lose a
loved one? If death brought down the curtain forever, then our love for
others would be a cruel joke, a passing feeling with no ultimate meaning.
But is it possible that cold, impersonal nature created us and evolved such
intimate feelings in us only to let us down in abject despair? Or is it more
likely that God made us with an intense love for others that would help
turn us, finally, toward our common Creator?

2 How would the ability to love others be a cruel joke if there was
nothing beyond this life? Explain. In what way does human love
point us to a Creator?

The reality and the strength of love is a more of what God is. Love is very real + very strong but is also difficult to define in human terms. These same traits — realism, and strength are true of God, who is also very difficult to describe. © Does God = Love? God is similar, but much more than Love

Christian Influence on Western Civilization

> *Blessed is the nation whose God is the LORD, the people he chose for his*
> *inheritance. From heaven the LORD looks down and sees all mankind; from*
> *his dwelling place he watches all who live on earth—he who forms the hearts*
> *of all, who considers everything they do. No king is saved by the size of his*
> *army; no warrior escapes by his great strength.*
>
> Psalm 33:12–16

The Christian moral foundation of social and cultural life brought
about sweeping benefits. Capitalism came into being in the West because

the Church recognized civil society must enjoy a rightful independence from its control. Benedictine monasticism embraced hard, physical labor as a means of knowing God. This gave a dignity to work that the world had never known before, a dignity that was later expanded through the Reformation and the Protestant work ethic. The Christian belief in reason—the very meaning of *Logos*—drove the scientific revolution. And Christian influence led to the establishment of the first universities, not just trade schools as had been the case in China, but communities of scholars where knowledge could be pursued because it was good for human beings to learn.

3 **What are some of the historical contributions of Christianity to the growth of Western civilization? Give some examples of how our postmodern culture is attempting to eradicate God and Christian heritage from the public arena.**

The Clash with Radical Islam and Secularism

Dear children, this is the last hour; and as you have heard that the antichrist is coming, even now many antichrists have come. This is how we know it is the last hour. . . . I do not write to you because you do not know the truth, but because you do know it and because no lie comes from the truth. Who is the liar? It is the man who denies that Jesus is the Christ. Such a man is the antichrist—he denies the Father and the Son.

1 John 2:18, 21–22

Reason alone, without faith, cannot deal with today's clash of civilizations. The problem in Islam is that it is a blind faith that neither supports reason nor is informed by it. The Allah of Islam is strictly a god of pure will whose dictates, as known through Islamic law, cannot be questioned. So we have a dilemma: in the West, reason alone without faith leads to chaos; in Islam, faith alone without reason leads to tyranny. And the tragedy is that the two sides can never find common ground.

4 Do you believe that Western civilization is at risk? Why or why not? Assuming you agree that our civilization is at risk, what role, if any, do you think the Church should take in response?

THE IDEOLOGY OF WESTERN CIVILIZATION IS THREATENED BY A LACK OF RESPECT FOR THE IDEALS WHICH HAVE BUILD IT. DEMOCRACY + THE VALUE OF INDIVIDUAL RIGHTS ARE CRITICAL + SUPERIOR SYSTEMS TO A MORE SOCIALIST, COLLECTIVIST WORLD VIEW. A CHRISTIAN WORLDVIEW LEADS TO GAINING MEANING FROM LIFE THROUGH LOVING GOD + LOVING ONES NEIGHBOR. AND LOVING THAT NEIGHBOR MEANS SEEING THEM AS AN INDIVIDUAL, SUPPORTING THEIR RIGHTS.

Renewing Western Culture

If my people, who are called by my name, will humble themselves and pray and seek my face and turn from their wicked ways, then will I hear from heaven and will forgive their sin and will heal their land.

2 Chronicles 7:14

G. K. Chesterton, author of the classic book *Orthodoxy*, explains why Christians are change agents. There are, he says, optimists and pessimists in the world. The optimists are always trying to do good things, and the pessimists are always wringing their hands in despair. But the Christian, he argues, is the only one with a balanced view — a pessimist because he knows that this is a fallen world and things do need fixing, but an optimist because he knows that God is all-powerful and in charge and that all things therefore can be fixed. If there's ever been a time in which renewal was essential, it is today when Christianity is pitted against not only hostile influences within Western secularism, but also against a massive, monolithic force, Islamofascism, that is pledged to destroy us.

5 To what extent is orthodox Christian faith the one source capable of renewing our culture? If Christian values are ultimately purged from our culture, as they have been across much of Europe, what do you think will arise to fill the void?

Proposition, Not Imposition

Dear friends, although I was very eager to write to you about the salvation we share, I felt I had to write and urge you to contend for the faith that was once for all entrusted to the saints. For certain men whose condemnation was written about long ago have secretly slipped in among you. They are godless men, who change the grace of our God into a license for immorality and deny Jesus Christ our only Sovereign and Lord.

Jude 3–4

Critics contend Christians are trying to "impose" their views on American life—in order to create a "theocracy," or a government run by the Church. But this is absurd; theocracy is contrary to the most basic Christian teaching about free will and human freedom. Christianity gave the very idea of separation of Church and state to the West. And Christianity advances not by power or by conquest, but by love. Christianity does not seek to impose, it proposes. The Gospel is the great proposal: Come to the wedding feast, one and all—black, white, rich, poor, East, West, Muslim, Jew, Christian—all are welcome, and it's never too late. God turns no man or woman away, not one. Through His Son, Jesus Christ, the Father brings us into His Kingdom.

6 In what way is "separation of church and state" actually an outgrowth of biblical Christianity? How is contending for God's values within a free society different from imposing a Church-run government?

Give unto Caesar - Separation .
1 man - 1 vote - Individuals have value
Free Will - Not Imposition

The End of History

But the day of the Lord will come like a thief. The heavens will disappear with a roar; the elements will be destroyed by fire, and the earth and everything in it will be laid bare. Since everything will be destroyed in this way, what kind of people ought you to be? You ought to live holy and godly lives as you look forward to the day of God and speed its coming. That day will bring about the destruction of the heavens by fire, and the elements will melt in the heat. But in keeping with his promise we are looking forward to a new heaven and a new earth, the home of righteousness.

2 Peter 3:10–13

Science has confirmed what the Scriptures teach, that history will end. One day it will end. History will not end when humanity reaches utopian goals, as some speculated in the 1990s, but when Christ returns in glory at the second coming. As C. S. Lewis says, the author of history, like the producer of a play, will step onto the stage, bringing down the curtain. No one knows the hour or the season when Christ will return, but there are signs of the providential direction of history. Many scholars agree that the return of the Jews to their homeland is a crucial sign of the fulfillment of the eschatological promise; an even more particular sign would be recognition of Jesus as the Messiah by many among God's chosen people. So depending on one's perspective, the place of Israel and our support for it becomes critical.

7 Do you believe that history as we know it will one day come to an end? On what do you base your answer, and how does it impact your worldview?

Christ Will Return

I saw heaven standing open and there before me was a white horse, whose rider is called Faithful and True. With justice he judges and makes war. His eyes are like blazing fire, and on his head are many crowns. He has a name written on him that no one knows but he himself. He is dressed in a robe dipped in blood, and his name is the Word of God. The armies of heaven were following him, riding on white horses and dressed in fine linen, white and clean. Out of his mouth comes a sharp sword with which to strike down the nations. "He will rule them with an iron scepter." He treads the winepress of the fury of the wrath of God Almighty. On his robe and on his thigh he has this name written: KING OF KINGS AND LORD OF LORDS.

Revelation 19:11–16

Christians believe that Christ will come back to earth. But this time He will return in glory and power, to judge the living and the dead and to make all things new. The Kingdom of God will finally be established then. We cannot fully understand this — we see only dimly now — but Christ's post-resurrection appearances and the Scriptures provide fascinating glimpses of what will happen when we are resurrected and reign with God forever. This is Christianity's ultimate hope and promise.

8 How will Christ's second coming differ from his first coming? How well are you prepared for it? How would you live differently if you knew exactly *when* Jesus would return?   194/187

- "Particular Judgement" of the Thief vs Common Judgement

- Prisoner steps onto Stage

?

Judgment and Hell

> *Just as man is destined to die once, and after that to face judgment, so Christ was sacrificed once to take away the sins of many people; and he will appear a second time, not to bear sin, but to bring salvation to those who are waiting for him.*
>
> Hebrews 9:27–28

> *Behold, I am coming soon! My reward is with me, and I will give to everyone according to what he has done. I am the Alpha and the Omega, the First and the Last, the Beginning and the End.*
>
> Revelation 22:12–13

All Christians believe that there will be a last judgment that will follow the second coming. The Athanasian Creed summarizes biblical teaching by saying that at the coming of Christ all men shall rise again "and shall give an account for their own works." There would not be the justice we all long for if God, the Perfect Judge, did not reward *and* punish. Even for believers, there will be judgment.

God doesn't want "anyone to perish, but everyone to come to repentance" (2 Peter 3:9). He promises that every individual who comes to Him in genuine faith and repents of his sins will be saved and spend eternity with God. But God gives each person a free will. Reluctantly, He respects the choice the person makes to remain alienated from Him while alive. He doesn't send the unrepentant person to hell; the unrepentant person chooses it.

9 In what way do people, by virtue of their free will, have the ability to choose hell rather than heaven? How will the judgment of the believer be different from the judgment of the unbeliever?

Christ's Kingdom Will Be Established

Then I saw a new heaven and a new earth, for the first heaven and the first earth had passed away, and there was no longer any sea. I saw the Holy City, the new Jerusalem, coming down out of heaven from God, prepared as a bride beautifully dressed for her husband. And I heard a loud voice from the throne saying, "Now the dwelling of God is with men, and he will live with them. They will be his people, and God himself will be with them and be their God. He will wipe every tear from their eyes. There will be no more death or mourning or crying or pain, for the old order of things has passed away."

Revelation 21:1–4

Christians believe that Christ will come back. But this time He will return in glory and power, to judge the living and the dead and to make all things new. The Kingdom of God which we know in Christ and His Church will finally be established. This is what is meant by the Old Testament expression, *shalom*. That word, used so blithely as a greeting, is translated as "peace." But shalom means much more than the absence of hostility; it means concord and harmony in society. Christ gives us His shalom to live with a measure of the blessedness or divine happiness that we will one day fully know when He returns to reign forever.

10 What is Christianity's ultimate hope and promise? What are some ways that Christ's kingdom will be different from this world? To what extent do you long for the day when Christ makes all things new?

The Joy of Orthodoxy

I seek you with all my heart; do not let me stray from your commands. I have hidden your word in my heart that I might not sin against you. Praise be to you, O LORD; teach me your decrees. With my lips I recount all the laws that come from your mouth. I rejoice in following your statutes as one rejoices in great riches. I meditate on your precepts and consider your ways. I delight in your decrees; I will not neglect your word.

Psalm 119:10–16

True Christians understand that the faith was given once for all and is filled with life and excitement. True Christianity is a logical and coherent explanation of reality. It begins with the rational premise *God is*. He is the ultimate reality. Why then is there suffering? Because God gave humans free will. We chose not to obey, so evil came into the world. Satan's control didn't stand, however. God invaded earth in His Son. The battle raged, and the Son was arrested and executed, as the payment for evil. But the stone was rolled away, and God raised Him from the dead, and with His resurrection guaranteed our own new life. The Holy Spirit was sent to finish the invasion, establishing Christ's Kingdom through His body, the Church. We can now exchange our lives for Christ's life. Reconciled with Him, we are reconciled with each other, living a holy life in community, defending life at every stage. One day Christ will come again and finally establish God's Kingdom. All those in Christ will enjoy God's fellowship eternally, as humankind was meant to from the beginning.

So how in the world do so many people these days talk about the Christian faith and its doctrines as being dry and brittle? You may say it's frightening, upsetting, life-changing, radical, extreme—but dull and boring, never.

11 **What has God most impressed upon you during your study of *The Faith*? How has your life been impacted in a way you did not expect?**

Consider Him Who Endured

Therefore, since we are surrounded by such a great cloud of witnesses, let us throw off everything that hinders and the sin that so easily entangles, and let us run with perseverance the race marked out for us. Let us fix our eyes on Jesus, the author and perfecter of our faith, who for the joy set before him endured the cross, scorning its shame, and sat down at the right hand of the throne of God. Consider him who endured such opposition from sinful men, so that you will not grow weary and lose heart.

Hebrews 12:1–3

There is a door by which all humans pass from darkness into the light. The way through it is narrow, the Doorkeeper tells us, but He promises to open the door and welcome us into His light. For He is the light by which everything else is enlightened, which is why the Christian faith is attractive and inviting; far from an imposition, the faith is the world's great hope. This door is still open today, but just ajar. This faith, which once built the greatest civilization in human history, must now engage in the titanic struggle of our times. Western culture is doing everything in its power to shut that door. But the Doorkeeper (who is the Door) will never allow it to fully shut. He invites you to pass through it.

✦ **12** How is orthodox Christianity an invitation to an exciting life of adventure? What steps will you take today to increase your participation in God's great drama? In what ways might this role bring you greater joy?

DVD Closing Segment and Prayer (5 minutes)

Use the space provided below to take notes on anything that stands out to you.

In the Coming Days

Choose one or more of the following ways to further digest and apply the concepts and principles you're learning:

- **Set aside some alone time to prayerfully reflect and meditate on the material covered in this session.** You might wish to review all of the summary sections preceding each question, or select the particular Scripture verses and corresponding synopsis you feel God is leading you to study. As you meditate and focus on God's Word, let his truth fill you. And as you pray and invite the Holy Spirit to transform and renew your mind, consider what God may be teaching you. What new insights have you discovered; what fresh perspectives have you gained; how might you apply these things to your everyday life? Use the space below to journal these things.

- **Meet with one or two other people from your group to further discuss how you might apply what you're learning to your everyday life.** Share with one another what has impacted you and how God is especially speaking to you. Discuss what concepts or topics have been particularly difficult for you to understand or accept. Also be sure to set aside some time to pray together.

- **Initiate a dialogue with someone who is not a participant in your group.** Invite a friend who is not yet a Christian to interact with you over some of the concepts you have been covering in the book, DVD clips, and group discussion. Be especially careful to listen with a sincere desire to hear and understand what your friend believes and why. Ask your friend if he or she would be interested in hearing some of the ways you've been impacted by your study of the material. You may wish to share some of the insights you gained from your conversation with the rest of your group at the next opportunity.

THE NICENE CREED

We believe in one God, the Father Almighty,
Maker of heaven and earth,
of all things visible and invisible (sessions 1, 4, 5).
And in one Lord Jesus Christ, the only begotten Son of God,
begotten of his Father before all worlds,
God of God, Light of Light,
very God of very God,
begotten, not made, being of one substance with the Father (session 4);
by whom all things were made;
who for us and for our salvation
came down from heaven,
and was incarnate by the Holy Spirit (sessions 2, 4)
     of the virgin Mary (session 2),
and was made man (session 2);
and was crucified also for us under Pontius Pilate (sessions 2, 3);
he suffered and was buried;
and the third day he rose again according to the Scriptures (session 2),
and ascended into heaven, and is seated at the right hand
of the Father (sessions 2, 4);
and he shall come again, with glory, to judge both the living and
the dead (sessions 4, 6);
whose kingdom shall have no end.
And we believe in the Holy Spirit, the Lord and giver of life,
who proceeds from the Father and the Son (session 4);
who with the Father and the Son together is worshiped and
glorified (sessions 4, 5);
who spoke by the prophets (session 1);
and we believe in the one holy catholic and apostolic church (sessions 3, 5);
we acknowledge one baptism for the forgiveness of sins (session 5);
and we look for the resurrection of the dead,
and the life of the world to come (session 6).

The Faith

What Christians Believe, Why They Believe It, and Why It Matters

Charles Colson and Harold Fickett

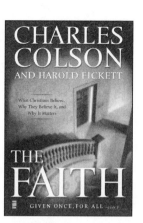

Rightly understood and rightly communicated, the Christian faith is one of great joy. It is an invitation to God's kingdom, where tears are replaced by laughter and longing hearts find their purpose and their home. This is the heart of the gospel: God's search to reclaim us and love us as his own. But have we truly grasped this?

Those of us who have disdained Christianity as a religion of bigotry — have we repudiated the genuine article or merely demonstrated our own prejudice and ignorance?

Those of us who are Christians — have we deeply apprehended the mission of Jesus, and do our ways and character faithfully reflect his beauty? From the nature of God, to the human condition, to the work of Jesus, to God's coming kingdom, and all that lies between, how well do we understand the foundational truths of Christianity and their implications?

The Faith is a book for our troubled times and for decades to come, for Christians and non-Christians alike. It is the most important book Chuck Colson and Harold Fickett have ever written: a thought-provoking, soul-searching, and powerful manifesto of the great, historical central truths of Christianity that have sustained believers through the centuries. Brought to immediacy with vivid, true stories, here is what Christianity is really about and why it is a religion of hope, redemption, and beauty.

Hardcover, Jacketed: 978-0-310-27603-6

Pick up a copy today at your favorite bookstore!

God and Government

An Insider's View on the Boundaries between Faith and Politics

Charles Colson

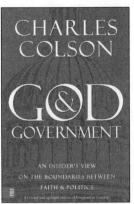

How should Christians live their faith in the public arena?

With a passion for truth and moved by the urgency of the times we live in, Colson has written God and Government, re-voicing his powerful and enduring message for our post-9/11 world.

In an era when Christianity is being attacked from every side — books being written charging Christians with being theocrats and trying to impose their views on an unwilling culture — what is the message of the Christian church? What does the Bible say, and what do we learn from history about the proper relationship between faith and culture? Appealing to scripture, reason, and history, this book tackles society's most pressing and divisive issues. New stories and examples reflect the realities of today, from the clash with radical Islam to the deep division between "reds" and "blues." In an era of angry finger-pointing, Colson furnishes a unique insider's perspective that can't be pigeonholed as either "religious right" or "religious left."

Whatever your political or religious stance, this book will give you a different understanding of Christianity. If you're a Christian, it will help you to both examine and defend your faith. If you've been critical of the new religious right, you'll be shocked at what you learn. Probing both secular and religious values, *God and Government* critiques each fairly, sides with neither, and offers a hopeful, fair-minded perspective that is sorely needed in today's hyper-charged atmosphere.

Softcover: 978-0-310-27764-4

Zondervan Legacy Series

Charles Colson on Politics & the Christian Faith

Four Sessions on Why Christians Must Live Out Their Faith, Promote Freedom, and Be Good Citizens

Charles Colson

From his time as counsel to President Richard Nixon to his years as commentator on the radio broadcast Breakpoint and his leadership of Prison Fellowship, Chuck Colson is uniquely qualified to provide an insider's perspective on today's pressing issues of faith and politics. This four-session DVD curriculum gives individuals or small groups the opportunity to hear neither a "religious right" nor a "religious left" perspective but balanced, clear, and biblically based thoughts on these important issues. Colson provides a great starting point for informed and thoughtful discussion and application to life in a political world on the following topics:

- Is America a Christian nation?
- Should Christians be in politics?
- What is America's church and state problem?
- Can politics save America?

DVD: 978-0-310-28687-5

Pick up a copy today at your favorite bookstore!

ZONDERVAN®
.com

Loving God

Charles Colson

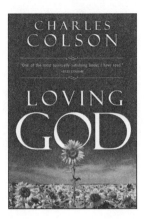

In his magnificent classic, Chuck Colson shakes the church from its complacency with a penetrating look at the cost of being Christian.

For those who have wondered whether there isn't more to Christianity than what they have known — and for those who have never considered the question — *Loving God* points the way to faith's cutting edge. Here is a compelling, probing look at the cost of discipleship and the meaning of the first and greatest commandment — one that will strum a deeper, truer chord within even as it strips away the trappings of shallow, cultural Christianity.

> "Looking for the complete volume on Christian living? This is it. And the title sums it up. If you desire life deep, rich, and meaningful, then it is simply Loving God."
>
> *Joni Eareckson Tada*
> *President, Joni and Friends*

Softcover: 978-0-310-21914-9

Pick up a copy today at your favorite bookstore!

ZONDERVAN®
.com

Share Your Thoughts

With the Author: Your comments will be forwarded to the author when you send them to *zauthor@zondervan.com*.

With Zondervan: Submit your review of this book by writing to *zreview@zondervan.com*.

Free Online Resources at
www.zondervan.com/hello

 Zondervan AuthorTracker: Be notified whenever your favorite authors publish new books, go on tour, or post an update about what's happening in their lives.

 Daily Bible Verses and Devotions: Enrich your life with daily Bible verses or devotions that help you start every morning focused on God.

 Free Email Publications: Sign up for newsletters on fiction, Christian living, church ministry, parenting, and more.

 Zondervan Bible Search: Find and compare Bible passages in a variety of translations at www.zondervanbiblesearch.com.

 Other Benefits: Register yourself to receive online benefits like coupons and special offers, or to participate in research.